ADVANCE PRAISE

Radical Roots makes an important contribution to the field of university-community engagement by chronicling and critically reflecting on the history and evolution of one institution's commitment to engage in deep mutually beneficial relationships with its local community as an anchor institution. The powerful legacy of Augsburg University – ahead of its time for embracing its role in, of, and with its urban community, and for embedding this commitment into its academic mission – is one that needs to be shared. Augsburg stands as a national exemplar for advancing the democratic mission of higher education by directly engaging its students, faculty, staff, and community partners in the practice of democracy. A must-read for all who are interested in strengthening university-community partnerships.

> *Rita Axelroth Hodges, M.S.Ed., Associate Director, Netter Center for Community Partnerships,*
> *University of Pennsylvania*

Radical Roots is an important and inspiring book. While telling the unique and compelling story of Augsburg University and the extraordinary impact of a faculty member, Joel Torstenson, on the institution, it has powerful lessons for higher education in general. Most centrally, *Radical Roots* illustrates the path to becoming a democratic civic university, which is dedicated to its local community and the values of democracy, social justice, and equity. In so doing, it makes clear why Augsburg is a national leader as an anchor institution, galvanizing academic, volunteer, and institutional resources for the mutual benefit of the university, the city, and the community. By vividly describing how Augsburg brought civic and community engagement into the very heart of the university, *Radical Roots* has made an invaluable contribution to our understanding of how higher education can fulfill its democratic promise.

Ira Harkavy, Ph.D., Associate Vice President and Founding Director of the Barbara and Edward Netter Center for Community Partnerships, University of Pennsylvania

In the midst of fiscal stress and political confrontations when higher education's commitment to the liberal arts and civic practice is fragile and yet so necessary, *Radical Roots* will provide the leaders and faculty members of colleges and universities with a profile of inspiration, intelligence, and resiliency. The Augsburg University story is a necessary antidote to institutional skepticism and a bright pathway to successful democratic education.

Richard Guarasci, President Emeritus, Wagner College & author, Neighborhood Democracy

This thoughtful volume makes three things clear. One professor can make a difference. Universities can stand for what matters most. And higher education still transforms lives.

Michael Lansing, Professor of History, Augsburg University

For those of us who believe deeply in the value of place-based collaborative work in rooting democracy, even and perhaps especially in the midst of national and global divisions and divisiveness, we can take heart from the saga described in this compelling volume, one played out over many decades at one of today's most effective anchor institutions in our higher education orbit. Critically, we witness here the evolving embedding of one professor's principles of democratic engagement as learning and public service intertwined into the very lifeblood of a university, opening the possibility for others across the years to fashion what it means to live at the "intersections of place and mission, location and vocation," for generations to come. The time span is instructive in teaching us all the patience needed, and the rewards to be garnered, if we can stick with the "radical roots" of those who saw so clearly how universities can truly be the public goods that our public so desires and yet so often questions today. The welcome thread of optimism runs clearly through this tale, grounded in real programs and practices only growing over time.

Nancy Cantor, Ph.D., Chancellor, Rutgers University-Newark

This book tells much of my story as a student in the Urban Studies program at Augsburg with both Joel (Torstenson) and then Garry (Hesser), tapping into my desire to experience a new model of learning...Such novel engagement in key learning methods propelled me toward a rewarding career, first as a community organizer (and)...later as a rural business banker and community developer...interdisciplinary perspectives as championed by Joel, was a cornerstone for my personal growth and success as a graduate of the Augsburg Urban Studies program.

Rick Bonlender, Augsburg Class of 1978

When I take stock of the institutions and experiences that have shaped my sense of what matters most, attending Augsburg towers above. This book, which is littered with people and programs at Augsburg that directly shaped my own sense of self and vocation—from Gary Hesser to Campus Kitchen to the Sabo Center—helps explain why I'm far from alone in feeling that way. *Radical Roots* not only documents the history of Augsburg's neighbor-centered approach to education, it also places it in vital broader conversations about the state of our democracy. There are rich lessons in this book for anyone trying to think through what it means to be a committed and responsible neighbor, and how to support others in becoming the same.

Chris Stedman, Augsburg Class of 2008, former humanist chaplain at Harvard University and director of the Yale Humanist Community, author of IRL and Faitheist, and writer and host of Unread

In addition to capturing the story of Torstenson, an influential academic leader who was before his time, this book also depicts a broader evolution in higher education and the changing ways we understand and carry out its public purpose. I was struck by the familiarity of the questions compelling students and colleagues to action in the late 60's and early 70's: To what extent is it wise, good, or even possible to retreat from the world to think and learn? Where does knowledge reside? Whose knowledge do we need to address the most pressing issues of our time? With vivid examples based in the specific place, mission, and faith tradition of Augsburg University, concepts such as the anchor institution, place-based learning, and civic agency come to life. It's an excellent case study, as well as a specific history. Also, as a HECUA alum and member of its board of directors during its final years, this story matters to me. In the wake of the COVID/COVID-19 pandemic, when we lost so many people and organizations, I appreciate that Paul Pribbenow and colleagues took the time to document the crisis colony project, which became HECUA and the subsequent experiential learning programs that critically shaped my education and so many others'. I hope this text informs the work of others, and the legacy lives on.

Sinda Nichols, Director, Center for Community and Civic Engagement, Carleton College

At a time when many colleges and universities are alarmed by the trend in higher education to move from transformational to transactional teaching and learning and struggle to discern their relevance for and future in society, this publication provides timely inspiration, guidance, and hope...The authors present Augsburg University as a model that can inspire other institutions of higher learning to reflect how specific mission and academic programs align with the values, needs, and priorities of the spaces within which they operate, educate students to be engaged in local and national democratic processes, and nurture the common good, which goes beyond the often superficial conversations in higher education about experiential learning, service-learning, and place-based initiatives.

Alexander Rödlach, Professor of Medical Anthropology, Creighton University

This book is an inspiring story of the enduring impact of a single faculty member on his institution, field, and community. It also deftly weaves connections across many important trends and concepts in higher education, including urban studies, experiential learning, the responsibilities of anchor institutions, democratic education, and citizen professionalism. Finally, it is a testament to Augsburg University's long standing commitment to building community relationships and preparing students for civic life.

> *Alex Lovit, Senior Program Officer and Historian, Charles F. Kettering Foundation.*

Radical Roots is a beautiful tribute to Professor Torstenson and his enduring impact on Augsburg University. With histories that are inextricably linked, the book provides readers with captivating insight into the transformation of Augsburg as a leading national model for the engaged university and how Professor Torstenson contributed to its path in getting there. Community-engaged scholars, students, partners, and all those committed to civic and community engagement will enjoy diving into Professor Torstenson's journey to develop new community-engaged academic programs, high-impact experiential learning, and dynamic partnerships. Today, Augsburg University is on the leading edge of higher education institutions holistically committed to the public mission, and *Radical Roots* inspires us all to take action!

> *Bobbie Laur, President, Campus Compact*

Radical Roots tells the story of Augsburg University and the power of one person to create a movement of transformation by linking education, community-building, and service to neighbors. Read it for the history and come away inspired by what is possible.

> *Valerie Holton, Executive Director, Coalition of Urban and Metropolitan Universities*

RADICAL
ROOTS

RADICAL ROOTS

How One Professor Changed
A University's Legacy

GREEN BOUZARD

KATHLEEN CLARK

TIMOTHY D. PIPPERT

PAUL C. PRIBBENOW

Myers
Education
Press

Published by Myers Education Press, LLC

P.O. Box 424 Gorham, ME 04038

Library of Congress Cataloging-in-Publication Data available from Library of Congress.

13-digit ISBN 978-1-9755-0620-9 (paperback)
13-digit ISBN 978-1-9755-0621-6 (library networkable e-edition)
13-digit ISBN 978-1-9755-0622-3 (consumer e-edition)

Printed in the United States of America.

All first editions printed on acid-free paper that meets the American National Standards Institute Z39-48 standard.

Books published by Myers Education Press may be purchased at special quantity discount rates for groups, workshops, training organizations, and classroom usage. Please call our customer service department at 1-800-232-0223 for details.

Cover Design by Design & Agency, Bella Barrientes, Casey Kreie, Eris Kochmann, Blaine Weber, and Valerie Yang

Book design by Design & Agency, Dan Ibarra, Eris Kochmann, and Blaine Weber.

Visit us on the web at www.myersedpress.com to browse our complete list of titles.

DEDICATION

This book is dedicated to the generations of Augsburg students who have been shaped by the radical roots of Joel Torstenson and those who followed in his footsteps.

TABLE OF CONTENTS

VIII

ACKNOWLEDGEMENTS

This book has been a labor of love for its four authors, each of whom cares deeply about how Augsburg University embodies a commitment to the intersection of vocation and location, mission, and place. Our efforts to honor the legacy of Professor Joel S. Torstenson and his radical roots have been supported by many colleagues.

This book includes contributions from the following current and former faculty, staff, and students at Augsburg University: Rachel Svanoe Moynihan, Matt Maruggi, Dan Ibarra, Christopher Houltberg, Ben Stottrup, Joe Underhill, Natalie Jacobson, Isaac Tadé, Steven Diehl, Emily Knudson, Ariel Gutierrez, and Kane Balance.

The authors are grateful for financial support for this project from generous donors, including Margie and Mark Eustis (through the President's Strategic Fund) and Mark Johnson (through the Torstenson Endowment). Peer reviewers Bobbie Laur, Rita Hodges, and Michael Lansing made helpful suggestions that strengthened our narrative. Stewart Van Cleve, the Augsburg University Archivist, was invaluable in our research. And we were most fortunate to work with Design & Agency, the undergraduate graphic design studio, staffed by Augsburg students and led by professors Christopher Houltberg and Dan Ibarra, who designed the book's cover and interior pages.

WHO WE ARE
AND WHERE WE STAND

This book is a testimony of those who laid the foundation for Augsburg University to be the place and the community that it is today. As we share the stories of Augsburg's past, we want to acknowledge the intersections of our embodied identities and our positionalities as authors reflecting that of mostly white, cisgender, heterosexual persons. We feel this is important to name and recognize as it has undoubtedly shaped our world-view. During this writing process, we have stayed committed to reading and reflecting in a critical way in hopes of avoiding causing harm in the stories we tell. And, given the historical con-text of this book project, we recognize that there are stories of individuals in this shared community at Augsburg that weren't equally recorded or shared.

We acknowledge the "place" we emphasize in this book in-cludes land that originally belonged to the Dakota peoples and was stolen from them. As Augsburg's Land Acknowledgment states, the Dakota "are still here today. We honor their wisdom about this place, their recognition that we are all part of the same creation. We share their sense of obligation to the larger community, including to future generations." [1] We are commit-ted to learning from our Indigenous neighbors how to care for our place.

In addition, we realize some of the language used in the past may not be consistent with the inclusive language of the present. We acknowledge many key characters in this narrative are themselves white and primarily male. This does not diminish their impact on their students, the university, and the wider community. Still, it does limit their understanding of the lived experiences of those they engaged with in various settings and circumstances.

We must do better to document our stories of the past and the present to shape the vision of our future. And we know that many of you share this passion. Thus, please join us in making a commitment to share the whole story of our universities as our sagas continue.

[1] "TRIO/Student Support Services," Augsburg University, accessed August 9, 2023, https://www.augsburg.edu/triosss/.

MORE INFORMATION AND RESOURCES

Augsburg University has created a website as a supplemental resource to this volume, which is kept up to date with resources connected to the Torstenson legacy. This website includes digitized versions of Torstenson's writings and scholarship, current resources on experiential education and place-based community engagement, and articles highlighting Augsburg's evolving role as an urban university walking with our neighbors. Visit www.augsburg.edu/radicalroots for more.

CEDAR-RIVERSIDE NEIGHBORHOOD

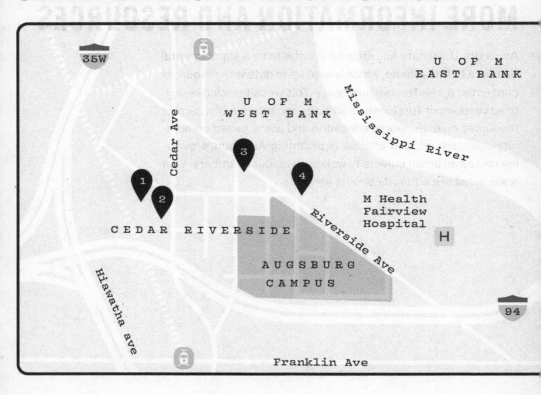

35W

U OF M
EAST BANK

Mississippi River

U O F M
WEST BANK

Cedar Ave

M Health
Fairview
Hospital

H

Riverside Ave

CEDAR RIVERSIDE

1

2

3

4

AUGSBURG

CAMPUS

Hiawatha ave

94

Franklin Ave

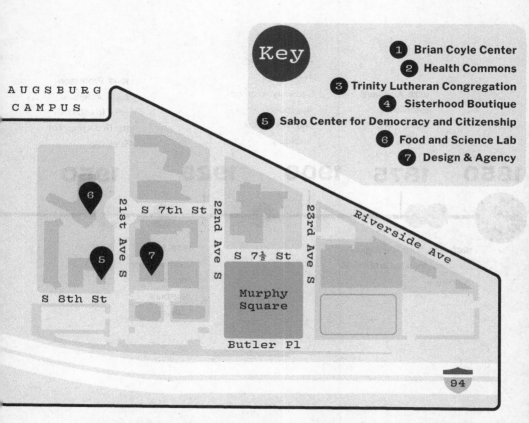

AUGSBURG CAMPUS

Key

1. Brian Coyle Center
2. Health Commons
3. Trinity Lutheran Congregation
4. Sisterhood Boutique
5. Sabo Center for Democracy and Citizenship
6. Food and Science Lab
7. Design & Agency

21st Ave S

S 7th St

22nd Ave S

S 7½ St

23rd Ave S

Riverside Ave

S 8th St

Murphy Square

Butler Pl

94

AUGSBURG UNIVERSITY CAMPUS

1916 Augsburg
Theological
Seminary renamed
Augsburg College
and Theological
Seminary.

1872 Augsburg
established
Minneapolis
campus

1947 Professor
Joel Torstenson
hired to establish
the Department of
Sociology

1850   1875   1900   1925   1950

1869 Augsburg Theological
Seminary founded in Marshall,
Wisconsin

1935 Joel
Torstenson
enrolled at
Augsburg
College

2020 Dr. Timothy D. Pippert, Professor of Sociology, named inaugural holder of Joel Torstenson Endowed Professorship, established with generous support from Mark Johnson, '75, who studied with Professor Torstenson

1971 Metro-Urban Studies Program founded (now called Urban Studies Program)

1971 Higher Education Consortium for Urban Affairs (HECUA) established

1967 Professor Torstenson's post-sabbatical report to the Augsburg University faculty, "The Liberal Arts College in the Modern Metropolis,"

1975

2000

2025

1963 Augsburg College and Theological Seminary renamed Augsburg College when the seminary merged with Luther Seminary in St. Paul.

1968 One Day in May

1968 Crisis Colony launched and offered to students

1977 Professor Garry Hesser hired

2006 Dr. Paul Pribbenow becomes the 10th president of Augsburg University

2017 Augsburg College renamed Augsburg University.

INTRODUCTION

"I use the term radical in its original meaning—getting down to and understanding the root cause. It means facing a system that does not lend itself to your needs and devising means by which you change the system."[1]

*Ella Baker, Civil Rights advocate and founder of the
Student Nonviolent Coordinating Committee (SNCC)*

This is the story of Joel S. Torstenson, born and raised on a farm in western Minnesota, who became a professor of sociology at his alma mater, Augsburg College (now Augsburg University). Torstenson embraced a radical vision of education that emphasized democratic engagement for his students and the society into which they graduated. Torstenson was radical in the same vein as Ella Baker, the renowned civil rights advocate and founder of the Student Nonviolent Coordinating Committee (SNCC), who believed deeply in the power of returning to the roots of systems in order to equip individuals to shape their own destinies and the communities in which they lived. Torstenson's vision of education was about expanding the horizons of learning and scholarship by focusing on shaping the agency of his students so that they were equipped to engage their fellow citizens in the work of democracy. It was a place-based education, deeply experiential in its pedagogy, and it transformed the curriculum and community engagement of the university. It took practical form in new academic programs such as social work, sociology, and urban studies, as well as in innovative experiential learning opportunities such as internships, service learning, and cooperative learning. It is a legacy that has transformed Augsburg over the past sixty years, and it offers lessons for the work of universities across the country who aspire to educate students for democratic engagement at the intersections of place and mission[2], location, and vocation. These are the radical roots that Joel Torstenson tended at Augsburg University.

These roots have their own history. In 1871, a small band of Norwegian settlers from Trinity Lutheran Congregation in the still tiny village of Minneapolis invited the fledgling remnant of a theological seminary in Marshall, Wisconsin, to come north to be an outpost for preparing preachers and teachers for the Lutheran immigrants of Minnesota. It was a humble beginning that has unfolded as an institutional saga with significant implications.[3] Little did they dream, those intrepid pioneers, that more than 150 years later, Augsburg University would be a thriving small university, educating students of diverse backgrounds and equipping them to live out their vocations around the world. Little did they dream, those faithful few, that this institution they helped survive in its early years, against all odds, would be an anchor in its urban neighborhood and an international model for linking education, community-building, and service to neighbors.

Our thesis is that Augsburg University's evolution as a community of learning suggests that all higher education institutions might find important resources for their lives by paying attention to the intersections of vocation and location, mission and place. Indeed, through these intersections, these institutions can discern best how to pursue their academic missions in the midst of a diverse and often turbulent world.

After more than 150 years, Augsburg is a university dedicated to the liberal arts, grounded in its Lutheran faith, and shaped by its distinctive location in the midst of an immigrant urban neighborhood. Augsburg's saga is one that has been tested repeatedly throughout the college's history, but as detailed below, it is a saga that abides because it is infused into the identity and character of the institution. It is the saga of an urban settlement, exemplifying the inextricable links between education, faith, place, and service to and with the neighbor.

The university has not always embraced Augsburg's saga as an urban settlement. Though location and place are central to the university's identity, it is not sufficient to explain the integrative power of the university's character. For that purpose, it is critical that place (understood not simply as geography, but also as a network of people, cultures, traditions, and environments) be seen through the lens of Augsburg's academic mission and work. This integrated view of place and mission required a new way of imagining the university's core work of educating students.

As Augsburg expanded its academic programs in the mid-twentieth century and more students enrolled, the institution touted the benefits of life in the city, including cultural resources, opportunities for work experiences, and so forth. But clear links between urban life and curriculum, for example, were not apparent as the college entered the 1960s.

Then entered an unlikely champion for a different vision of Augsburg's mission and identity. Dr. Joel Torstenson, a 1938 graduate of Augsburg, originally came to the college from his hometown in rural Minnesota. Joining the Augsburg faculty in 1947, Torstenson, a social scientist, began systematically expanding the college's academic programs in the social sciences and social work. This certainly brought students and faculty into contact with urban life and realities, but that contact remained limited to particular departments until Torstenson returned from a sabbatical in 1966, which transformed his thinking about the promise of "The Liberal Arts College in the Modern Metropolis."

In an address to the Augsburg faculty in 1967, Torstenson argued that his decision to study the role of colleges in the modern metropolis was influenced by the emerging understanding that cities were a dominant community reality in society, that

Augsburg was uniquely situated to develop an educational program responsive to this emerging reality about cities, and that Augsburg had much to learn from what other urban higher education institutions had done to integrate their locations into an academic program.

This momentous address included a myriad of practical recommendations for Augsburg to embrace its urban context as a "laboratory for liberal learning and research." From the most simple and pragmatic, such as hiring faculty who have a particular interest in urban issues, to curricular innovations such as a Metro-Urban Studies (now Urban Studies) program, to encouraging staff and faculty to live in the surrounding neighborhoods, to engaging with community advisors and partners, Torstenson's twenty-four-page address reads like a map to Augsburg fully embracing its location as classroom and context for a distinctive academic vision.

This, then, represents the critical turning point in Augsburg's saga, as the college integrated urban location and academic mission in ways that infused the commitment to the city into everything the college said and did. Augsburg History Professor Carl Chrislock, on the occasion of the college's centennial in 1969, suggested that Augsburg's new commitment to the city was a response to an academic revolution underway in the mid-twentieth century focused on new ways of learning about humans and society. Augsburg President Oscar Anderson, writing during that centennial year, claimed that the city is an "unlimited laboratory where students and their teachers, through work-study programs, now have the opportunity to observe first-hand what textbooks have implied from afar." While some institutions, Anderson continued, might choose to retreat behind ivied walls, "Augsburg chooses to be of the city."[4]

The lessons from Augsburg's saga for other communities are grounded in the work of integrating mission and location. It's not enough to say we are in this place, we must be able to say with conviction, we are of this place. It is about infusing all we say and do with this mission-based embrace of our place in the world. This connection of mission and location was undeniably catalyzed by the contributions of Joel Torstenson.

The purpose of this book is twofold. The first is to document and celebrate the radical legacy of Professor Joel Torstenson and to understand the impact of this legacy's inception, evolution, and current manifestations and impact at Augsburg and in the wider world. Professor Torstenson cared deeply about the public purpose of higher education, and Torstenson's model for what this public purpose might look like prompted a massive trans-formation in Augsburg University's trajectory. The resulting experiments in education and commitment to the city flowered into a legacy that has spurred Augsburg University to create an innovative model for 21st Century education. This model has impacted everything from student learning and community life, to teaching and curricular structure, to the public mission of the institution and its presence in the city and world. Torstenson's creative work in the 1960s and 1970s has been carried through the decades by continued innovation in teaching and learning based in experiential education, and a commitment to place and community building. This legacy has simultaneously advanced the public purpose and mission of the university.

Secondly, this book aims to share what are some of the lessons learned from more than sixty years of innovation following Torstenson's vision, with the hope that these lessons might serve the broader community of colleges, universities, faculty, staff, and students engaged in similar pursuits. Augsburg's innovative experiential education, place-based community engagement, and public and anchor institution work has been and will continue to be a model for other institutions. We believe that Torstenson's legacy, and the lessons learned through the years of its evolution, has lessons to teach and models to follow for our sibling institutions across the United States.

The story we aim to tell is one of an extraordinary man and those who carried on the vision of his work; of Augsburg's remarkable students, faculty, and staff and their commitment to experi-ential learning, social change, and accompaniment; and of an institution whose leadership has, over and over, committed to the public and democratic purpose of an institution in the heart of the city. The following chapters cover decades, starting with Torstenson's extraordinary life in and out of the classroom, and exploring his innovative work at Augsburg in Chapter 1. Torstenson's own writing on the purpose and possibility of a college being in and with the city can be found in Chapter 2, in his essay entitled, "The Church Related College in the City." Chapter 3 moves on to the contributions of Torstenson's successor, Garry Hesser, whose creativity, leadership, and dedication to experiential learning brought Torstenson's legacy into the 21st Century. Chapter 4 explores various ways Augsburg's distinct mission and identity have led to creativity in community-based learning and strong relationships in the neighborhood surrounding Augsburg, as well as three examples of innovation in experiential education across diverse disciplines. Chapter 5and 6 turn to an outgrowth of Torstenson's legacy: the democratic purpose of higher education. How has Augsburg been a place that has cultivated civic agency amongst its students, faculty, and staff so that their education, work, and daily living enliven the capacity to work together to act on all sorts of collective problems? What is the future of the democratic purpose of higher education in light of Augsburg's unique journey? Each section is followed by a series of questions to prompt further reflection, inviting readers to ask about how the lessons learned at Augsburg might inform the important work at other colleges and universities committed to advancing their missions in conversation with their places.

How can the lessons and legacy of the past sixty years inspire a brighter, more engaged, and more vibrant future? How can we all learn from the radical vision of Joel Torstenson what it means to educate agents of equity and justice in our democracy? How can we embrace the challenge of reinventing democracy in every generation through the education we offer our students at the intersections of vocation and location, mission and place? These are the questions that we propose to address in this story of Joel Torstenson and those who bear his legacy of education for democracy.

ENDNOTES

[1] Ella Baker, "The Black Woman in the Civil Rights Struggle," speech given at the Institute of the Black World, Atlanta, Georgia, 1969, https://awpc.cattcenter.iastate.edu/2019/08/09/the-black-woman-in-the-civil-rights-struggle-1969/

[2] Although Augsburg's mission statement has been updated regularly since the 1960s, it is summarized in the motto: "Education for service." The current mission statement states that "Augsburg University educates students to be informed citizens, thoughtful stewards, critical thinkers, and responsible leaders. The Augsburg experience is supported by an engaged community that is committed to intentional diversity in its life and work. An Augsburg education is defined by excellence in the liberal arts and professional studies, guided by the faith and values of the Lutheran church, and shaped by its urban and global settings." (Adopted in 2010)

[3] Throughout this volume, we use Burton Clark's definition of saga: "An organizational saga is a collective understanding of a unique accomplishment based on historical exploits of a formal organization, offering strong normative bonds within and outside the organization. Believers give loyalty to the organization and take pride and identity from it. A saga begins as strong purpose, introduced by a man (or small group) with a mission, and is fulfilled as it is embodied in organizational practices and the values of dominant organizational cadres, usually taking decades to develop." Burton Clark, "The Organizational Saga in Higher Education," *Administrative Science Quarterly 17*, no. 2 (June 1972): 178.

[4] Quoted in Carl Chrislock, *From Fjord to Freeway* (Minneapolis: Augsburg College, 1969), 235.

REFERENCES

Baker, Ella. "The Black Woman in the Civil Rights Struggle." Speech given at the Institute of the Black World, Atlanta, Georgia, 1969. Accessed July 31, 2023. https://awpc.cattcenter.iastate.edu/2019/08/09/the-black-woman-in-the-civil-rights-struggle-1969/.

Chrislock, Carl. *From Fjord to Freeway*. Minneapolis: Augsburg College, 1969.

Clark, Burton. "The Organizational Saga in Higher Education." *Administrative Science Quarterly 17, no. 2* (June 1972): 178–184.

The Genesis Of
The Torstenson Legacy

CHAPTER 1

Takk for Alt, *Professor Torstenson:*
How the Work of Professor Joel S. Torstenson
Shaped Augsburg University's Relationship
With Minneapolis

In his ninth decade, Dr. Joel S. Torstenson (1912–2007) began writing his memoir. The title, *Takk for Alt: A Life Story,* translates into "Thank You for Everything: A Life Story."[1] In this same spirit of appreciation, Augsburg University owes a debt of gratitude to Professor Torstenson.[2] The foundation laid by Augsburg's founders carved a path for Torstenson's radical vision of education to take hold in the 1960s and 1970s, a vision that continues to shape the institution's identity, focus, and mission. Augsburg has a unique relationship with the city of Minneapolis and our neighbors, which is due in no small part to his efforts. By examining our saga, we invite readers at other institutions of higher education to consider how their past continues to shape their future at the intersections of vocation and location, mission and place.

For anyone even remotely familiar with college marketing materials, it is obvious that every institution claims to be unique, and many also claim to be the most adept at preparing students for the world beyond a college campus. Perhaps there is some truth in each of these claims when particular aspects of a college are examined, but most claims of uniqueness are akin to believing that your institution holds the key to critical thinking skills. There are, however, some institutions that stand out in comparison to their peers. In recent years, Augsburg has garnered national recognition for groundbreaking work in service-learning[3] and experiential education, as well as support for students across an amazing array of backgrounds. This small Lutheran university in the heart of Minneapolis's Cedar-Riverside neighborhood is not only the most diverse private institution of higher education in the Midwest, it regularly receives attention for its support of students in recovery, those needing classroom accommodations, military veterans, LGBTQ+ students, women's athletics, students that have aged out of foster care, first-generation college attendees, and more.

Figure 1.1
Map of Cedar Riverside Renewal Area (March 1, 1968). Hennepin County Library

Augsburg can claim its status as a truly unique institution not simply based on recent accolades, but due to the institution's foundation, which actively discouraged following the path of

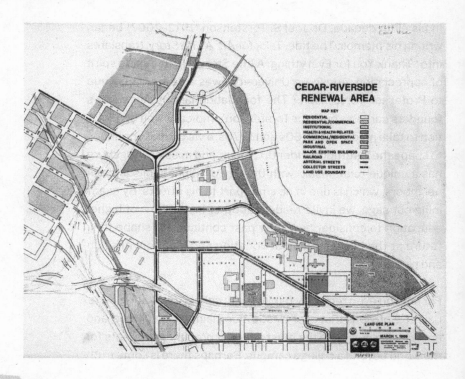

most universities. Augsburg's founding principles allowed pioneers like Professor Joel S. Torstenson to significantly impact the pedagogical practices of faculty, the institution's organizational structure, and how relationships were formed with Minneapolis residents, organizations, and government entities. This chapter will outline how the foundational aspects of Augsburg University and Joel Torstenson's leadership in the mid-1900s helped to transform Augsburg from a seminary in the country, to a college in the city, to a college of the city, and finally to what we have come to recognize as a university with the city.[4]

AUGSBURG'S FOUNDATION
SMALL TOWN ROOTS

When reflecting on the group of Norwegian settlers from Trinity Lutheran Congregation in Minneapolis inviting Augsburg Theological Seminary from Marshall, Wisconsin, to Minneapolis, Augsburg University's tenth president, Paul C. Pribbenow, expressed that it would have been impossible for the founders to have known the future of Augsburg. Even though the institution's founders would likely not have been able to envision the path Augsburg would take, the foundation they laid encouraged a distinct route that was based on expanding educational opportunities for immigrants rather than the more common practice of privileging a college education for the wealthy. Augsburg University's meager beginnings and emphasis on egalitarian educational opportunities unfortunately foreshadowed the institution's long-term financial challenges. While the ways in which Augsburg has navigated financial uncertainty is a topic beyond this book, it is related in the sense that many innovations sparked at the university were, and continue to be, based on the desire to do the most with few resources. This pattern began in 1869.

According to Carl H. Chrislock's book, *From Fjord to Freeway*, on the history of Augsburg University's first 100 years, Augsburg Theological Seminary was approved at the June 1869 Annual Conference of the Scandinavian Augustana Synod in Moline,

Illinois.[5] The trustees were authorized to purchase an already constructed school building in Marshall, Wisconsin. Reverend August Weenaas, who was called from Norway to teach at the Augustana College and Theological Seminary the year prior, was elected as the first president of Augsburg Theological Seminary. According to Chrislock, President Weenaas complained about inadequate financial support and the difficulty of hiring faculty from the beginning, but things quickly worsened. During the 1870 annual conference, the Scandinavian Augustana Synod was divided into two groups, one Swedish and the other Norwegian, with a small representation of Danish Lutherans. While the Swedish group held, the Norwegian and Danish branch quickly split into the Conference of the Norwegian-Danish Evangelical Lutheran Church in America and the Norwegian Augustana Synod. President Weenaas and the Augsburg Theological Seminary became part of the Conference of the Norwegian-Danish Evangelical Lutheran Church in America, but the Norwegian Augustana Synod contingency forced Weenaas and his theologians out of the school building in October 1870.

In what was actually Augsburg's first Crisis Colony (see later section on the 1968 Crisis Colony), President Weenaas housed around a dozen of the twenty students at his home and found housing around Marshall for the remaining students. Without other options in the small town of Marshall, Mr. Cooper, a local farmer, offered his small attic to serve as the Augsburg Theological Seminary. During much of the year, President Weenaas did not receive a salary, and at the end of the spring term, he gathered the students to inform them that the seminary would need to close.[6] As will be the pattern for at least the next 150 years, the Augsburg community banded together and refused to let that happen. A move, however, was in order.[7]

HEADING WEST AND BREAKING FREE

During the summer 1871 Conference of the Norwegian-Danish Evangelical Lutheran Church in America, Minneapolis was chosen over Madison, Wisconsin, for Augsburg Theological Seminary's new home. Preparing a site for the seminary on the outskirts of a milling village did not go off without a hitch. While significant donations of land, building materials, and money were promised, worries surfaced that St. Anthony Falls might fail. Since the falls powered the milling industry, they were the economic lifeblood of the entire region. As a result, only a fraction of the donations materialized. In yet another example of working through challenging times, Trinity Lutheran Congregation Pastor Ole Paulson borrowed $60 from Karen Danielson, whom Chrislock referred to as "a young servant girl," to start construction.[8]

While the earliest years set the stage for the necessity of resourcefulness, Augsburg's foundation was truly established when classes began at the new Minneapolis campus on September 15, 1872. The laying of the foundation for the Original Old Main was symbolic of how the campus would grow and change. It was built with the understanding that it would need to expand, and by 1875 it had more than doubled in size. The mission of the institution also expanded during this time.

Even though the Seminary remained the central mission of the institution, a three-step educational plan was devised in 1874. The three steps included the seminary where future ministers were trained, but also a college to prepare students not ready for the seminary, and an academy to prepare students not quite ready for college. According to Professor Phillip C. Adamo's book, *Hold Fast to What is Good: A History of Augsburg University in 10 Objects*, Augsburg's founders rejected the ivory tower type of education, instead understanding education to be a practical endeavor. The foundation of Augsburg established the goal of preparing preachers, teachers, farmers, and business owners that would be able to serve the Norwegian Lutheran immigrants of Minnesota and Wisconsin.[9]

President Weenaas was a strong presence for this educational expansion, but his recruitment of two professors from Norway, Sven Oftedal and Georg Sverdrup, fundamentally changed the tenor of Augsburg. Professors Oftedal and Sverdrup also led a movement that impacted the way thousands of Lutherans worshiped in the upper Midwest. According to President Bernhard Christensen, "Professor Georg Sverdrup was unquestionably one of the greatest theologians as well as one of the most inspiring teachers who have worked among Scandinavian Lutherans in America."[10] Oftedal and Sverdrup were both scholars and members of the Haugean movement (Haugeanism).

Hans Nielsen Hauge (1771–1824) was a lay preacher in Norway, a position that was deemed illegal as religious meetings not authorized by the Church of Norway were not allowed. Not only did he believe that ministry should not be confined to only those with seminary training, he and his followers understood that the church should be free of interference from the state. In addition, Haugeans also believed in the importance of congregational independence and, quite controversially, the obligation of the church to be involved in social life and human welfare.[11]

This movement was brought to the United States by Norwegian immigrants, including Oftedal, Sverdrup, and later the parents of Professor Joel Torstenson. The Haugean traditions were not universal among Lutherans in the late 1800s, ultimately leading to a rift in the wider church conference. When Augsburg moved to Minneapolis, it was part of the Norwegian-Danish Evangelical Lutheran Church in America. In 1890, they joined with two other Lutheran organizations to form the United Norwegian Lutheran Church in America (UNLC). The merger sparked a fierce battle between Augsburg College and St. Olaf College as to which institution should be the official college of the church. It was decided that St. Olaf would serve as the official college and Augsburg would serve as the official seminary.[12]

In response to what was viewed as an injustice on the Augsburg campus, Friends of Augsburg was formed by Sverdrup to help protect Augsburg College and Seminary from losing more autonomy to the UNLC.[13] In a series of court cases and expulsions of pro-Augsburg congregations, *The Lutheran Free Church* (LFC) was formed in 1897.[14] Augsburg's fifth president, Bernhard Christensen (1938–1962), reflecting on the LFC around its fiftieth anniversary, wrote, "ever since that time the activity and interests of Augsburg and those of *The Lutheran Free Church* have been closely and constantly intertwined. Augsburg Seminary has, in fact, often been fittingly spoken as the 'heart' of our church body."[15] The Haugean tradition, then, shaped Augsburg Seminary and College as well as the independent congregations that left the UNLC for *The Lutheran Free Church*, in the formation of a free church of free congregations in a free land.[16] Lutheran Free Church principles such as congregational independence, the involvement of lay leadership, the openness to engaging in dialogue with other religious traditions, the importance of education, and a commitment to addressing problems of human welfare continue to this day to impact the mission of Augsburg University. According to Christensen, "I believe that there are a number of things in the history of *The Lutheran Free Church* which indicate that our founding fathers never proposed that there should be any attempt on the part of members of congregations to escape from social and political obligations."[17]

The foundation built by Augsburg's founders was so strong and so impactful that the following is how Carl Chrislock chose to conclude his book, *From Fjord to Freeway*:

> Some advocates of experimental innovation believed their course to be consistent with Augsburg's earliest traditions, the school's retreat into isolation during its middle period notwithstanding. Sven Oftedal and Georg Sverdrup were sensitive to the plight of disadvantaged groups within American society and keenly conscious of the psychological lift provided by ethnic self-esteem. They were profoundly critical of the Norwegian and Norwegian-American establishments of their day. The two young professors also tried new teaching methodologies—the early examination system, for example—in an effort to help the students discover their own identity. Both emphatically rejected ivory tower concepts of education, believing that institutions of learning should relate organically to the communities (or congregations) that they ostensibly served. (1969, 236)

Professors Georg Sverdrup and Sven Oftedal ultimately served as the second (1876–1907) and third (1907–1911) presidents of Augsburg, continuing to shape the institution in a way that expanded access to higher education. According to Chrislock, Sverdrup and Oftedal challenged the educational standard that held up "the cultivated gentleman trained in Greco-Roman studies as the ideal type."[18] Chrislock also explained that Sverdrup and Oftedal disdained pedagogies which produced professionals separated from the people, and argued that learning should be connected with living experience rather than preoccupied with "glossaries, citations, and crammed memories."[19] In a speech given to graduates in 1884, President Sverdrup noted that at many colleges, "the aim appears to be the stuffing of knowledge into youth as one pours peas into an empty sack...where the teachers are eloquent and the students inarticulate...where everything is communicated but little or nothing is absorbed. At such schools, the rule was 'Never think! Learn instead to conform to the prevailing code and you will succeed.'"[20]

In 1911, Georg Sverdrup's son George became Augsburg's fourth president (1911–1938), expanding the educational offerings to include an education that was more suited for general life in the world with the goal of attracting a broader range of students. He also presided over the institution in 1921 when the long-established goal of expanding educational opportunities finally included women. At this point, the transition from a seminary with an attached college to a college with an attached seminary was well underway. It would, however, take several decades for Augsburg University to become racially integrated.

"SIN CITY"

The markers of the ideas and ideals of Presidents Weenaas, Sverdrup, Oftedal, and G. S. Sverdrup remain entrenched in the way Augsburg serves students today, but that is not to suggest that the foundation remained consistently strong. When Augsburg chose to relocate from Marshall to Minneapolis, the campus was isolated from the village and operated quite autonomously. Minneapolis would not stay small for long, and soon the expansion of the city made some faculty, students, and alumni nervous.

The way Augsburg University practices civic responsibility today is a far cry from the 1920s. In that era, Augsburg felt called to fight against the expansion of taverns and dance clubs in the neighborhood.[21] When this was unsuccessful, Augsburg began to isolate itself from the community. It was not difficult for the students to isolate themselves from the neighborhood because Cedar-Riverside was not their home. Most students at the time were from rural Minnesota and had come to Augsburg based on their membership in The Lutheran Free Church.

In 1922, Augsburg Seminary graduate, successful entrepreneur, and president of Augsburg's Board of Trustees, Knut Birkeland, devised a plan to save Augsburg from the ills of the approaching city. He spearheaded the creation of the Augsburg Park Association to purchase a wooded, 40-acre, parcel of land in Richfield. Part of the land was to be subdivided and sold as residential lots to fund the building of a new Augsburg campus on the shores of Wood Lake. There were several reasons Birkeland and others saw the need for Augsburg to relocate, such as industrial smoke and the commercial expansion of the area. According to Philip Adamo, the author of Augsburg's sesquicentennial history, the reasons were also grounded in white flight. In his book, Adamo references a pitch for Augsburg Park in *The Lutheran Free Church Messenger*: "The old neighbors, who were supporters of our school, have moved away to more desirable locations, and their place has been taken by a more or less undesirable class of people of varied race and color."[22] The plan was for Augsburg to sell its location in Minneapolis and within a few years, "the school would be operating in a new plant on a spacious campus surrounded by congenial Scandinavian neighbors, and including a substantial contingent of LFC adherents."[23]

Augsburg lore is that while the move to Richfield was supported by a large contingency and given serious consideration, ultimately, the desire to remain in the city was a clear and decisive

11

decision based solely on the understanding that the city was where Augsburg could do its best work. It appears that this was not entirely the case as the "decision" took decades to make, involved poor sales of the residential lots, the Great Depression, Birkeland's unsolved murder, diverted storm water drainage, and the threat of eminent domain.[24]

The legend of Augsburg making a united stand to remain in the Cedar-Riverside neighborhood shades the fact that the foundational principles of the institution seemed to be weakening. Augsburg ultimately made a strong commitment to its urban location, but that commitment did not come for quite some time. For decades, the institution purposefully insulated itself from the neighborhood and remained so until the foundation could be repaired and prepared for expansion by Joel S. Torstenson and a supporting cast of faculty, church leaders, community partners, and college presidents. Before connecting his work at Augsburg University from 1947 to 1977, Professor Torstenson's roots must be examined.

TORSTENSON FOUNDATION
A KIND BOY WITH POPULIST ROOTS

In his memoir, Joel S. Torstenson wrote, "Perhaps one of the most indelible memories of my mother's love for me was her frequent expression, *"Du er en snil gut, du* Joel" (you are a kind or good boy, Joel)."[25] While a sweet sentiment between mother and son, it also identifies one of the reasons Professor Torstenson was able to be such an effective agent of change. Regularly described as kind, thoughtful, and intelligent, he was not assumed to be a threat, nor a radical. Even though he pushed to radically change existing social structures and redefined education to emphasize democratic engagement, his kind demeanor, education, race, gender identity, social class, and religion provided him with opportunities not available to most. This thread will be expanded upon later in this chapter, but this brief section intends to demonstrate that when he arrived at Augsburg, he came with a strong foundation geared toward social justice and building community.

Born in 1912, Joel was the youngest of ten Torstenson children, with four brothers and five sisters. He grew up on the family farm on the banks of the Lac Qui Parle River in western Minnesota, but his memoir focused little on the farming operation. When reflecting on his early years, his focus was on the importance of family and community.

Countering the idea of isolated family farms charting their own path, Torstenson understood the importance of community support. His nearest neighbors were family, and the local community, related or not, was thoroughly involved in supporting each other's work. According to Joel,

> all of these relations with both our neighborhood and the life and work of the surrounding villages and towns involved our family in personal and social as well as economic and political linkages with the larger society surrounding our family farm. All these contributed to our preparation for sharing in the emerging common life and culture of a growing American society. Perhaps the popularized concept of the 'family farm dream' with its emphasis on rugged individualism and economics provided an inadequate account of what life was really like in these early farming settlements, one that has neglected the important socio-cultural values associated with rich neighborhoods and surrounding community experiences and associations.[26]

He also described the seeds for his lifelong focus on social justice. According to Torstenson, his parents were influenced by the Haugean movement in Norway. As he explained in his biography, "one of the reasons for the success of the movement was attributed to the fact that it 'combined a political struggle for the farmers (bonder) against the official classes with the strong emotions engendered by a religious revival. In other words, the movement was both 'populist' and 'pietist.'"[27] The Torstenson parents brought these influences when they immigrated to America, providing Joel and his siblings with strong examples of political activism. While Torstenson outlined his mother's political influences, he details the efforts of his father and brothers in his memoir. Torstenson family members were actively involved in supporting rural electrification and telephone service, local cooperatives, *The Lutheran Free Church*, Minnesota Farmer-Labor Party politics, aid to Norway after the 1940 Nazi invasion, and the Farmers Union. Torstenson also mentioned the community's participation in the Farm Holiday Association.[28] In addition to fighting for the rights of farmers, the Farm Holiday Association helped to organize local citizens to stop farm foreclosure sales during the Depression. The larger the crowd, the more likely the sheriff would have to postpone the sale. According to Torstenson, "Knowing many of the participants in these populist protest activities, I witnessed close hand and with sympathetic understanding these dramatic social forces at work in our community."[29]

When Torstenson first left his family farm, he drew on his strong foundation of activism and democratic principles. Given that he graduated from Dawson High School during the Depression, his options were limited. He decided to enroll in the one-year rural elementary education certificate program at Moorhead State Teachers College. During the program, he was exposed to democratic principles of education that he could apply throughout his career and which helped shape the learning opportunities of today (a topic which will be further discussed in later chapters). In his first teaching position, he earned $65 a month to teach twenty-two students across multiple grades, all from Norwegian American families.[30] On his first day as a teacher, he wrote on the board in gold chalk, "I'll help you and you'll help me, then what a wonderful school this will be."[31] To Torstenson, that was not a cordial greeting, but an indication that he was going to organize a structure to democratically determine the norms for behavior in the classroom. According to Torstenson, "it truly reflected my personal predilection toward the democratic ethos that I had been nurtured in from my childhood."[32]

THE FIRST STOP AT AUGSBURG

After three years of teaching near his family's farm in rural Minnesota, Torstenson enrolled at Augsburg in 1935. He worked his way through school, completing a B.A. in history and a minor in social science in 1938. In the 1939 Augsburg yearbook, the *Augsburgian*, it is noted that the class of 1938 selected Joel S. Torstenson to represent them at commencement. At that time, Torstenson was described as "a truly representative student..." with "...an enviable record in the field of scholarship... active in Forensics, Publications, and those clubs having to do with contemporary social and political problems..."[33]

While pursuing his undergraduate studies at Augsburg, the stage was set for him to become a college professor. During his senior year, President George Sverdrup died unexpectedly. Torstenson's favorite professor, H. N. Hendrickson, became the acting president, and Hendrickson asked Torstenson to take over his European History course. This ultimately led to Torstenson pursuing his M.A. in history with a minor in sociology at the University of Minnesota. In his memoir, he commented that Professor Hendrickson "was apparently pleased with my performance, since to my great delight, he asked me to continue teaching the course the following year while I pursued my post-graduate work in history at the University of Minnesota."[34] According to Torstenson, the unanticipated turn of events resolved his uncertainties about the future as he was free to continue his academic pursuits while being a member of a college faculty.

COOPERATIVE FARMING AND WORKING FOR PEACE

In 1939, Torstenson married Francis (Fran), who proved to be equally political and interested in social change.[35] The two became deeply involved in the peace movement during World War II. They joined the local Fellowship of Reconciliation (FOR) chapter.[36] They were attracted to FOR's ecumenical, anti-war, and pro-peace orientations based on social justice, love, and reconciliation. As their participation in FOR grew, they looked for ways they could live their lives committed to peaceful human relations.

In Torstenson's words, "the more we thought about the merits of a cooperative and community-oriented culture and its relevance for our FOR position, the more we began thinking about what next steps we might take in promoting such a culture."[37] They reacted by forming a cooperative farm, Bass Lake Farm, with their friends, Elliot and Eleanor Marston. According to Torstenson, since he was teaching part-time, he also had time to work on the eighty-acre dairy and poultry farm about ten miles northwest of Minneapolis.[38]

Bass Lake Farm had several initiatives, which widened the Torstensons's social contacts and solidified their focus on social justice. They became actively involved in the larger cooperative movement, and both Torstenson and Marston served as board members of the Summer Field Co-op Grocery Association in North Minneapolis, an interracial co-op. The main goal of their farm, however, was not to sell milk and poultry. Instead, the primary goal was the promotion of peace. During the life of the farm (1940–1945), efforts were spent hosting interested visitors to educate them on the peace movement. In addition, the farm housed conscientious objectors and individuals waiting for alternative service work assignments. At the end of World War II, these functions ceased, and the sudden death of Elliot Marsen forced the sale of the farm. For the next two years (1945–1947), Torstenson began working as the Director of Education and Community Relations for an Association of Cooperatives in southeast Minnesota and northeastern Iowa. The new position required a move to Lanesboro, ending his ability to remain on the faculty of Augsburg University. However, this detour turned out to only be temporary.[39]

TRANSFORMING AN INSTITUTION

In the summer of 1947, Professor Torstenson received a letter from Dr. Bernhard Christensen, Augsburg's fifth President (serving 1938–1962), asking him to return to Augsburg to develop a major in sociology and a program of social work education. In the fall of 1947, he returned to Augsburg to establish the Department of Sociology and resume his graduate studies, earning a Ph.D. in sociology from the University of Minnesota with a minor in history in 1958. According to Professor Torstenson:

My return to Augsburg in the fall of 1947 was destined to be the beginning of my major life's career as a college professor and academic scholar. For the next thirty years, I was immersed in the college's dynamic growth and development as a liberal arts center of higher learning seeking to respond creatively to the complex challenges of a rapidly changing world.[40]

As noted earlier, Augsburg had become increasingly insulated from its surrounding community. The foundation laid by Presidents Weenaas, Sverdrup, and Oftedal, in which pedagogical innovation and expanding educational access were central components, was showing fatigue. However, with the support of Presidents Bernhard M. Christensen (1938–1962) and Oscar Anderson (1963–1980), Professor Torstenson began his work as the most radical professor in Augsburg's history, grounding the institution in the importance of location and place. He was able to effectively rebuild Augsburg's foundation as well as allow for its ultimate expansion because he operated using the principles similar to Ella Baker's understanding of being radical—facing a system that does not lend itself to your needs and devising means by which you change the system.[41] He also found success as a changemaker because of his personal characteristics. As a kind-hearted (*Dr er en snil gut, du* Joel), suit-wearing, highly educated, white male whose efforts were grounded in Christian principles, he possessed the cultural capital to be radical in his actions while avoiding the negative label. Important changes to the curriculum, organizational structure, and relationship to the city of Minneapolis that Professor Torstenson instigated helped Augsburg to transform from a college in the city, to a college of the city. The foundation he built was so strong that future leaders like Professor Garry Hesser and presidents Charles S. Anderson (1980–1997) and William V. Frame (1997–2006) continued the momentum in a way that allowed President Paul C. Pribbenow (2006–present) to ultimately envision Augsburg as a university with the city.

BUILDING A CURRICULUM FOR CHANGE

Upon arrival in 1947, Professor Torstenson set to work on developing a comprehensive sociology and social work curriculum with the primary objective of helping students attain a better understanding of society. In so doing, he hoped that departmental alumni would become effective agents of social change. In his words:

> In developing the department of sociology, I consciously sought to promote a rigorous and dispassionate, as well as a sympathetic understanding of society, the human community, and personality. I thought it important for both student and teacher to wrestle with the tension between a 'rigorous and dispassionate' quest for societal understanding, and the more 'compassionate and sympathetic' concern for the fate of the human community. It was in the context of such an encounter that I sought to promote lively classroom discussions of issues of social justice, human dignity, and

caring concern for all members of the human community. This, I thought especially appropriate in the context of Dr. Christensen's emphasis upon education for service. Closely related to this approach was my interest in examining the relevance of Christianity for effective social service.[42]

He also practiced and encouraged introducing students to community leaders and using the community as a learning laboratory to educate both students and professors. As he explained, "For all learners, but especially for the professor, this meant becoming participant observer-learners in such significant community affairs that would have special relevance for the subjects being studied."[43]

Building on these goals and teaching practices, he established courses on topics never offered at Augsburg University. He tapped his rural roots and offered a rural sociology course, but most of the curriculum he built focused on issues germane to life in the city. In addition to introductory courses to both disciplines of sociology and social work, he started courses on racial and intercultural relations, urban sociology, social psychology, sociological theory, and public welfare. He also oversaw the development of a field experience requirement that was the precursor to Augsburg's robust internship program. He was so successful that for much of the 1950s, the sociology department had the most majors on campus.[44]

Professor Torstenson's curricular innovations continued throughout his tenure and he seemed to seize almost every opportunity or national event to help students understand the world they inhabited. He developed far too many courses to list them all, but a few examples demonstrate how he shared his interests and expertise with students. About the time he enrolled at Augsburg as a student, the Minneapolis General Strike (Trucker's Strike) of 1934 was taking place. His interest in the strike ultimately led to his involvement in church-labor relations during the 1950s, examining and advocating for organized religion and church-related colleges playing roles in labor struggles. Out of that experience, he added a course on industrial relations to the sociology curriculum, in which labor leaders were regular guest speakers. He also developed courses around the United States Bicentennial, New-Town development projects and construction of Cedar-Riverside Plaza, and even a tour of western American cities that coincided with a choir tour. In the spring of 1964, he presented a series of six televised lectures during the Minnesota Private College Hour series on the local Twin Cities public television station. The series was titled, "Religion and Race in American Life." According to Torstenson, "I attempted to give a scholarly documentation of the role that religion had played in America's historic dilemma caused by the wide gap between its dramatic creed and racist practices."[45]

In addition to his curricular innovations, he helped establish the Augsburg Social Science Research Center. The creation of the research center was an indication of the direction Professor Torstenson was guiding the department. As a member of the Advisory Committee of the Urban Life Commission of the National Lutheran Council, he was asked by the director in 1964 to begin a campus area study in the Twin Cities. It was the first time a comprehensive sociological analysis of the community surrounding Augsburg had been conducted. Later, he was asked to repeat the assessment in St. Paul's east side Phalen Park community. These first studies became the impetus for the creation of the research center. He hired Robert W. Clyde to direct the center where he "accepted assignments on specific urban problems, not only as a service to the community but also in the belief that such research was adding to the total corpus of social science knowledge."[46]

Interest in both sociology and social work grew, with students majoring in either sociology or social work within the confines of the department. Professor Torstenson understood that despite the popularity of his department, people were often unable to distinguish between the two disciplines. According to Chrislock, he became frustrated when sociology was equated with social work, implying that "his department's sole preoccupation was to turn out well-meaning 'do gooders' equipped with as much professional social work training as could be squeezed into an undergraduate college curriculum."[47] It was also important to Torstenson that, as practiced in the sociology department, "education for service" did not equate to charitable assistance to those who are disadvantaged. Professor Torstenson and his colleagues also recognized the need for a more applied focus for students wanting to pursue social work. While the move was not sudden, approval was granted in 1974 to form the Department of Sociology and Social Work (formally the Department of Sociology). Soon after, accreditation requirements led to the creation of a separate Department of Social Work.

PROGRESSIVE LEADERSHIP

The departmental organization and curriculum development guided by Professor Torstenson did not occur in a vacuum. He fostered such change at Augsburg because he was not alone in his call for social change and the importance of utilizing the richness of the college's physical location. Professor Torstenson was able to radically change the institution because the original foundation laid by Presidents Weenaas, Sverdrup, and Oftedal encouraged progressive thinking and innovation from future leaders like President Bernhard M. Christensen (1938–1962).

While still in its insular state when Professor Torstenson joined the faculty, there were indications that Augsburg would soon be going in a different direction. Torstenson praised President Christensen as a leader that pushed Augsburg to respond to the changing realities of life, with the motto, "Education for Service." Christensen was invited to join Mayor Hubert Humphrey's Council on Human Relations, and he served as chair from 1948–1950. In that role, he helped complete the Minneapolis Self-Survey of its human relations practices and the fight against discrimination.

All of Professor Torstenson's participation in civic, social justice, and church-related organizations are too numerous to mention, but of great importance was his role as the Augsburg University delegate to the Joint Committee for Equal Opportunity in the mid-1950s. The Joint Committee was composed of representatives of over sixty civic organizations in the Twin

Cities with a focus on eliminating discrimination in the fields of employment and housing. He was elected chair of the Joint Committee in 1958. His leadership in the Joint Committee led to his role as the secretary and chair in the early 1960s of the Fair Housing Committee of the Greater Minneapolis Council of Churches. The committee created a letter campaign, sponsored large inter-church gatherings, conferenced with legislators, and used local media to push anti-discrimination in housing legislation. His work on the Fair Housing Committee led to his being invited by Mayor Arthur Naftalin to join the Mayor's Commission on Human Relations in 1963.[48]

Around that time, Augsburg University had a change in leadership, but not a change in the level of support for Professor Torstenson's efforts. Augsburg's connection and commitment to the city of Minneapolis grew under President Oscar A. Anderson (1963–1980). Under Anderson's leadership, Augsburg began to embrace its location in the city, began recruiting underrepresented students, and expanded the campus infrastructure, signaling that Augsburg belonged in the Cedar-Riverside neighborhood. According to Adamo, at a time when most college presidents were calling in the National Guard to quell student protests over civil rights or the war in Vietnam, "Anderson responded with calm and grace, even defending Augsburg students as people of conscience when outside critics attacked them."[49] President Anderson openly demonstrated his support for the Civil Rights Movement in many ways, most notably in 1965, when he addressed the approximately 800 students assembled for chapel services, stating, "Today, John Louma and I are going on a walk."[50] John Louma was the student body president and the two led the entire group from Si Melby Gym on campus to Hennepin County Courthouse in a demonstration of support for civil rights. Adamo argues that that moment is when Augsburg University began to more fully embrace its Minneapolis location.[51]

KEYS TO THE CITY

One of the most obvious signs of support from President Oscar Anderson was the granting of an extended sabbatical to Professor Torstenson. During the 1965–66 academic year, Torstenson studied what should be the role of a liberal arts college located in an exploding metropolis. He began by drawing on classic works from sociologists like Emile Durkheim, Karl Marx, George Simmel, Ferdinand Tönnies, and Max Weber to frame the increasingly rapid transformation of societies from rural to primarily urban. In his report, he charted population projections in the United States from 1900 to 2000, citing that at the time of his writing over two-thirds of Americans lived in areas defined by the Census as Standard Metropolitan Areas. Torstenson also drew from his contemporaries like Hans Bloomfield, John Dyckman, Scott Greer, and Robert Nisbet to explain the current state of the modern metropolis as well as scholars like Charles Dobbins, Eugene Hohnson, George P. Smith, and Willis Rudy to address the ongoing transformation of higher education.[52]

As a proponent of experiential learning, Torsten's research was not limited to what he could find in the campus library. During his sabbatical, he visited fourteen colleges and universities to assess what leaders in the field were doing. He criticized the practice of many universities that deliberately isolated themselves, their campuses, and their intellectual endeavors in rural areas. While those in pastoral settings believed they could avoid the social and economic realities of urban centers, institutions like the University of Pennsylvania, University of Chicago, Case Western Reserve University, Columbia University, and other institutions located in metropolitan areas similar to Augsburg University had to rethink their relationship with the community. Upon returning to Augsburg, he presented his post-sabbatical report to the Augsburg University faculty in 1967. His report, "The Liberal Arts College in the Modern Metropolis," can be found in the supplemental website for this volume.[53] According to President Paul C. Pribbenow (2006–present), "Torstenson's twenty-four-page address reads like a map to Augsburg fully embracing its location as a classroom and context for a distinctive academic vision."[54] With the support of President Anderson, Professor Torstenson's report became a guide for refocusing Augsburg University. No longer comfortable with its insularity, Augsburg fully embraced Minneapolis as a laboratory for liberal learning, research, and as an opportunity for community service.[55] Seeing the city as a laboratory meant to Torstenson that Augsburg faculty, staff, and students should learn about the inequalities playing out in the city and should not ignore the realities facing city residents.

Included in Professor Torstenson's report were eleven recommendations for action the college should undertake in capitalizing on what he understood as the unique opportunities based on Augsburg's status as a liberal arts college in the Cedar-Riverside neighborhood. In introducing the recommendations, Torstenson pointed out that Augsburg, like most urban colleges, had unfinished work before maximizing its location in the heart of a metropolis. He hoped that his recommendations would "...serve as a stimulus to discussion which in turn may lead to actions much better thought out than these are at this stage."[56] It was in that spirit that he offered the following recommendations to the Dean of the College:[57]

"Augsburg should establish a task force on college and metropolis."

"In the recruitment of new faculty, the college should seek to draw to its teaching staff people who are interested in and concerned about the college's role in the modern metropolis (of course this cannot be a substitute for scholarly competence)."

"The college ought to explore the possibilities of adding a limited number of courses to its curriculum which reflect its concern for urban affairs."

"An interdisciplinary program on Man in the Metropolis should be developed."

"Efforts should be made to expand the field experience programs into areas beyond those developed for students enrolled in the courses in education and social work."

"An expanded student employment service might be developed which takes more complete advantage of the urban setting."

"The college ought to carefully determine the format and type of annual public programs it should foster."

"Efforts should be made by the College to get as many of its faculty living within walking distance of the campus as possible."

"The extra-curricular programs at Augsburg should be carefully examined in terms of maximizing the College's location."

"In the field of Community Relations, Augsburg Faculty and Administration (perhaps through the Faculty Senate) should give careful study of the imagery the college wishes to have reflected; the media it wants especially to use; and the particular publics it wants to cultivate."

"As another means of building bridges between Augsburg's Academic Community and the life of the metropolis around it, advisory councils made up of leading alumni and other people engaged in particular vocations and pursuits should be created who could meet occasionally with representatives of students and faculty of appropriate departments in the college."

Torstenson argued that whatever role colleges and universities seek to play in society, they must do so in the context that the metropolis has become the dominant community in modern society. In his memoir, he commented that he was pleased that the college eventually acted on most of his recommendations. For example, his work led to the establishment of the Metro-Urban Studies Program (now Urban Studies) in 1971.[58] The program, as designed by a student-faculty team headed by Torstenson, was a college-wide interdisciplinary program that continues to serve as a model for examining a topic from various perspectives.

Professor Torstenson's inspiration went beyond the establishment of a new program and impacted the overall framing of the college. Inspired in part by his report, Augsburg faculty and Board of Regents approved the Academic Blueprint for Augsburg University in 1970. The blueprint stemmed from an institutional self-study and included four basic presumptions that would lead the college through the 1970s and beyond. Concerning Augsburg's position as a college of the city, the blueprint stated:

Augsburg College should develop the greatest educational benefit from its urban location and should contribute to the enrichment of the life of the city. The College recognizes that the city is simultaneously a most important educational resource, an appropriate context for the College's participation in the life of the community, and, itself, a most timely object of study.[59]

All told, Torstenson's recommendations sparked initiatives that ultimately helped Augsburg become nationally recognized in experiential learning and commitment to urban communities. They also helped prepare the university for the steps it would take in responding to what was referred to in the late 1960s as the "urban crisis."

RESPONDING TO AN "URBAN CRISIS" AND ASSASSINATION

As is clear from Professor Torstenson's description of what he strove to provide students in his sociology courses, national events were always part of the discussion. That practice, and his existing work on issues of race and discrimination, helped him serve as one of the campus leaders in how Augsburg would participate in the Civil Rights Movement. In talking about his involvement, Torstenson stated:

> In a general way, many of us at the college sought creative ways to respond to the new challenges—each out of the context of his or her particular social geography. For me, the crisis of the sixties came to have a compelling relevance for my work at the college. Everything I had learned from my studies there, including a compassionate concern for human welfare and social justice, prompted my involvement in the civil rights movement.[60]

Torstenson cited US President Lyndon Johnson's February 28, 1968, "Special Message to the Congress on Urban Problems," in which he detailed the "crisis in the cities" as a call for Augsburg to act. According to President Johnson:

> Today, America's cities are in crisis. This clear and urgent warning rises from the decay of the decade—and is amplified by the harsh realities of the present...People who could afford to move out by the hundreds of thousands to new suburbs to escape urban crush and congestion. Other hundreds of thousands were trapped inside by a wall of prejudice, denial, and lack of opportunity.[61]

Locally, this decline was playing out with unrest and aggressive policing in north Minneapolis, especially in the summer of 1967.[62] While considering how Augsburg might involve itself in working toward social change, President Oscar Anderson held what has been described as an impromptu meeting of several faculty in the spring of 1968.[63] The timing of the meeting was important, as it prompted Augsburg's response to the assassination of the Reverend Dr. Martin Luther King, Jr.

According to Professor Torstenson, continuing Augsburg's educational practices without change would be indefensible given the tragic events unfolding locally and nationally. As such, several campus-wide initiatives were sparked. One example was "One Day in May," when all classes were replaced by a series of lectures and workshops by faculty and leaders of the local Black community.[64] The topics discussed included racism, power, politics, and forms of resistance, giving the opportunity for Augsburg students, faculty, and staff to "listen to the voices of despair and revolt from the inner cities of Minneapolis and St. Paul" following Dr. King's assassination.[65]

With today's lenses, such an event might be open to the criticism that it is not the responsibility of the disenfranchised to teach everyone else about their struggles, but it was groundbreaking for the time and helped solidify an even deeper commitment to the community by Augsburg. In reflecting upon the 50th anniversary of the event, former Pan-African Student Services Director Hanu Dinku explained that the event shed light on systemic white supremacy in the Augsburg community and the nation. This public acknowledgment created a level of transparency and accountability that helped move Augsburg in the right direction.[66] Soon after, Augsburg students followed the lead of other institutions and created the Black Student Union.

According to Torstenson, Augsburg had been partially prepared for the work that needed to be done because President Bernhard M. Christensen brought "education for service" into alignment with Augsburg's relationship with the city of Minneapolis.[67] In Torstenson's view, this allowed President Oscar

Anderson to respond more effectively:

When the so-called "urban crisis" came, this positive support for "community service and good human relations" had left its mark upon both the College's curriculum as well as its general orientation as a college in the city. During the turbulent sixties, with the vigorous support of its new president, Oscar Anderson, the College articulated its orientation more explicitly and developed new programs to implement its emerging urban consciousness. By the end of the sixties, this consciousness had been both publicly affirmed and internally adopted as one of the official policies of the College.[68]

CRISIS COLONY

One of the boldest attempts to connect with the community and educate Augsburg students on challenges facing their neighbors was the establishment of the Crisis Colony.[69] Just like students at Augsburg, leaders of the American Lutheran Church's Youth Department felt called to action. Reverend Ewald (Joe) Bash had worked to help students from Lutheran colleges explore interracial and ethnic issues, so a partnership between the two institutions, guided by Joe Bash and Joel Torstenson, was formed.

According to Bash, students at the time held three major concerns.[70] They hungered for social justice, community, and an education that linked them to society and community. In addressing those issues, the Crisis Colony experiment started with eighteen students from across the country living communally on the north side of Minneapolis for eight weeks in the summer of 1968. Students took classes, heard from speakers from local organizations, conducted individual internships, and worked on projects as a group. They also discussed their experiences on campus and at local churches.

Torstenson and Bash's pedagogical innovation could also be seen in how learning was understood as a totality that included experience, that students were involved in the creation of knowledge, and the absence of grades (pass-fail). According to

Professor Garry Hesser, the way Torstenson and Bash designed the Crisis Colony "reflected the reemerging affirmation of the work of John Dewey and others who insisted upon a new episte-mology and the relevance of experiential education."[70] This type of co-learning model, based on the understanding that students were also responsible for creating knowledge, was recognized as possible at the graduate level, but was viewed as seemingly (and incorrectly) too difficult at the undergraduate level at the time. Bash and Torstenson were also innovative regarding the use of community experts. The speakers were often paid and considered visiting professors as Torstenson and Bash under-stood the immense value of their contributions.

Based on the success of the first run, a second iteration of the Crisis Colony followed during the spring quarter of 1969. Living in the community for an entire term gave students more time to become involved. In addition to morning seminars each day with Augsburg professors, students had individual assignments in the community and also had shared goals such as supporting a local political campaign, voter registration drives, and assist-ing in the organization of public housing residents. They also led several worship services at area congregations and presented at a higher education conference. Far ahead of their time, the students also participated in groups working toward police reform.

Like many of Professor Torstenson's other ventures, the Crisis Colony lived on in various fashions for decades. After the sec-ond colony, it became clear that the experiment was taking too many of the university's resources to be sustainable. To address the costs as well as the importance of the colony, Augsburg Uni-versity Dean Kenneth Bailey convened representatives from several institutions in the upper Midwest to explore an inter-col-lege partnership. As a result of the deliberations, the Higher Education Consortium for Urban Affairs (HECUA) was created in 1971, with Professor Torstenson serving as the first director. HECUA ran future colony programs, becoming a permanent program in different forms as the "Semester in the City," then the Metro Urban Studies Term (MUST), and most recently the

"Inequality in America" program. Later, Professor Torstenson contributed to the growth of HECUA by establishing the Scandinavian Urban Studies Term (SUST) at the University of Oslo in 1973.[71]

Given the pedagogical innovation and sustainability of the program, the creation of the Crisis Colony provided significant benefits to the participants. In its early stages, it was a product of its time. When considering the Crisis Colony with today's perspectives, especially some of the reactions from the student journals, some things might make readers rightfully uncomfortable. For example, the use of "colony" strikes too close to the long history of colonizing peoples on their own lands. When reading the rationale of Bash, however, it becomes apparent that they were using the term colony to differentiate a style of education that differs from what was taking place on college campuses. "The Colony receives definition from the encounter with the questions of the community to which it has come."[72]

The name of the program is not the only problematic component that surfaces when critically reflecting on past practices. The colonies, while not exclusively white, were mostly so. As aptly described by one of the participants in the second colony, "The Crisis Colony is an effective way for a person from a background like mine with limited contact with the problems and troubles of inner-city living to learn to respect the values and attitudes of these people."[73] Given the lack of diversity at Augsburg and the other institutions sending students to Minneapolis neighborhoods at the time, it cannot be ignored that dated, paternalistic terminology was used in describing the neighborhoods and that white kids were being educated about racism through the labor of others. Still, like most of Torstenson's work, his ideas were also far ahead of their time. The use of participant observation, formation of community partnerships, deeply valuing the role of community experts, and the collective creation of knowledge are all aspects still valued in education at Augsburg today.

Ultimately, what Professor Torstenson did throughout his career was to shift where the "lessons" were coming from. He was amazingly consistent in his approach to education, helping students co-create knowledge, engage in experiential learning beyond the classroom, express the importance of the city in our daily lives, and draw from the wisdom and expertise of community experts. It is those lessons that have helped Augsburg to grow even more in its quest to be an equitable institution. His work made it possible for President William V. Frame, Augsburg's ninth president, and President Paul C. Pribbenow, Augsburg's tenth president, to bring the voices that Torstenson had to seek out into the campus community, not as guest speakers, and not even as "welcomed others," but as the community.

CONSTANT TRANSFORMATION

In 1977, Torstenson reached the mandatory retirement age at the time, but he did not slow down. He traveled to Norway, continued to assist the efforts of HECUA, did research at the University of Oslo, co-wrote a book on urbanization and community development in Norway (1985 publication), and wrote a document outlining Trinity Lutheran's response to the changing Cedar-Riverside community. In his work with Trinity Lutheran Church, the congregation that invited Augsburg to Minneapolis in the 1870s, he helped organize the purchase of Block 185 as part of neighborhood revitalization. The block sits on Riverside Avenue, adjacent to Augsburg University's northwestern boundary. As a congregation, they funded the construction of thirty-five apartments and seventeen townhouses, with Joel and Fran living in the complex for several years. According to Torstenson, the project was honored by the Minneapolis Environmental Commission as "one of the most beautiful and creative neighborhood revitalization projects in the city."[74]

Following the example of Professor Torstenson, Augsburg University has not let transitions, mandatory or not, slow it down. As an institution, Augsburg is constantly working to be a more equitable and democratic institution. Examining the complexity of Professor Torstenson's legacy leads us to better understand how our actions today will eventually be interpreted. We believe we are being innovative and that we have a handle on our short-comings, but we are likely short-sighted in both of those areas. With that understanding, the following chapters, including a 1974 address Torstenson gave to the American Lutheran Church Faculties Conference, serve to link the past with the present initiatives of the university.

One of the themes of Professor Torstenson's legacy that helped guide his approach to teaching and learning was that education and the overall work of a university is an evolving process. What we are doing today, with the best intentions and based on current pedagogy of teaching and learning or best practices, has a shelf life. We may look back in a decade on what we have lifted up in this book and find examples of how we should have done things differently. Instead of shying away from that reality, this book embraces the concept of constant transformation. By focusing on lessons Augsburg faculty, staff, and administrators have learned along the way, this book demonstrates the reality of what the institution has learned from Professor Joel S. Torstenson: keep innovating, keep engaging, and most importantly, keep listening.

The legacy of constant transformation, for both Professor Torstenson and Augsburg, is demonstrated in the following chapter. Torstenson had shaped countless institutional policies and written extensively before writing The Church Related College in the City, but the paper holds specific significance. The paper was written in 1974 with retirement on the horizon for Professor Torstenson. By that point in his career, he had shaped countless institutional policies and written extensively about Augsburg's role in the city, allowing him to reflect on over a quarter-century of accomplishments. His work, however, was mostly directed toward and consumed by the Augsburg community.[75] By presenting the paper to the October 1975 American Lutheran College Faculties Conference, Torstenson created a public record of his work at Augsburg while also demonstrating to other American Lutheran colleges what is possible when institutions of higher education embrace the opportunities of life and learning in the modern metropolis.

ENDNOTES

1 Joel S. Torstenson, *Takk for Alt: A Life Story* (Minneapolis: Self Published, 2004).

[2] Augsburg Theological Seminary was founded in 1869 in Marshall, Wisconsin. The institution relocated to Minneapolis, Minnesota in 1872. In 1916, the name was changed to Augsburg College and Theological Seminary until the Seminary merged with Luther Theological Seminary in 1963. On September 1, 2017, Augsburg College became Augsburg University, which better reflected the complexity of the organization. With the exception of direct quotes, the institution will be referred to as Augsburg University, or simply Augsburg, regardless of the time period being referenced.

[3] "Service-learning is a teaching and learning strategy that connects academic curriculum to community problem-solving...students and participants learn and develop through active participation in thoughtfully organized service that...meets the needs of a community...helps foster civic responsibility; and that is integrated into and enhances the academic curriculum of the students...and provides structured time for students or participants to reflection on the service experience ("Service Learning," Youth.gov, accessed January 13, 2023, https://youth.gov/youth-topics/civic-engagement-and-volunteering/service-learning). Today, scholars and practitioners have critiqued and expanded on the term "service-learning." Terms such as "service learning and community engagement (SLCE)," "community-based learning," "community-engaged learning," "community-engaged research," "critical service-learning," "place-based community engagement," and the broader term "experiential education" are today used interchangeably with the term service-learning. See Chapters 3 and 4 for more on the evolution of Augsburg's engagement in service-learning and expanded modalities. In general, the term can be understood in this book to mean a form of experiential education that engages holistically with community partners, and includes co-learning models, ongoing volunteerism, research, or other community involvement connected to coursework for mutual benefit of all involved.

[4] According to Professor Garry Hesser, Joel Torstenson always considered his work as "with" the city and its residents.

An examination of Professor Torstenson's efforts, especially in the Crisis Colony, make that abundantly clear. The language of the institution and past presidents, however, has been focused on "in" and "of" the city.

[5] Carl H. Chrislock, *From Fjord to Freeway: 100 Years - Augsburg College* (Minneapolis, MN: Augsburg College, 1969).

[6] In honor of Mr. Cooper, several locations on the Minneapolis campus have been designated "Cooper's Attic" over the years.

[7] Chrislock, *From Fjord to Freeway.*

[8] See Phillip C. Adamo, *Hold Fast to What is Good: A History of Augsburg University in 10 Objects* (Minneapolis, MN: Split Infinitive Books, 2019), for an interesting discussion about Karen Danielson.

[9] Adamo, *Hold Fast.* It is important to note that Augsburg's efforts to serve Norwegian Lutheran immigrants were made possible due to the forcible removal of Native peoples from their lands. This is part of our story, as is the fact that many of those trained in the early days of Augsburg would have engaged in work that served to eradicate Native cultures through forced education and conversion to Christianity. Since the 1970s, Augsburg has responded to the fraught history of the land now occupied by the University. In 1978, Augsburg established the American Indian Student Support Program (AISSP) to provide support for Native students attending Augsburg. The University also created an American Indian Studies program, which later became an academic major. In addition, the University offers full tuition scholarships for Native students, and has supported a variety of regular Native cultural events on campus, as well as supporting the Native student association. For additional insights on Augsburg's response to the historical treatment of Native people in Minnesota, see Eric Buffalohead, "Augsburg University Land Acknowledgement: A Case For More Than Mere Words." Unpublished manuscript, Augsburg Univer-

sity, 2023.

[10] Chrislock, *From Fjord to Freeway*, 317.

[11] Bernhard Christensen, "The Idea of *The Lutheran Free Church*" in *The Lutheran Free Church*, ed. Eugene L. Fevold (Minneapolis: Augsburg Publishing House, 1969), 316–330.

[12] Chrislock, *From Fjord to Freeway*.

[13] "Lutheran Free Church. 1897-1963," St. Olaf College, accessed August 22, 2022, https://pages.stolaf.edu/locluth/lutheran-free-church/.

[14] "History," Association of Free Lutheran Congregations, accessed August 22, 2022, https://www.aflc.org/about-us/history-of-the-aflc/.

[15] Christensen, "The Idea of *The Lutheran Free Church*," 316.

[16] St. Olaf College, "Lutheran Free Church."

[17] Christensen, "The Idea of *The Lutheran Free Church*," 328. Augsburg University has been affiliated with the Evangelical Lutheran Church in America (ELCA) since 1988.

[18] Chrislock, *From Fjord to Freeway*, 26.

[19] Chrislock, *From Fjord to Freeway*, 26.

[20] Chrislock, *From Fjord to Freeway*, 96.

[21] Dancing was not allowed on campus until 1965.

[22] Adamo, *Hold Fast*, 39–40.

[23] Chrislock, *From Fjord to Freeway*, 150. LFC stands for Lutheran Free Church.

[24] See Chapter 3 in Philip C. Adamo's *Hold Fast to What is Good: A History of Augsburg University in 10 Objects* for an interesting examination of Augsburg Park.

[25] Torstenson, *Takk for Alt*, 17.

[26] Torstenson, *Takk for Alt*, 25.

[27] Torstenson, *Takk for Alt*, 20.

[28] In the same way President Franklin D. Roosevelt declared a National Bank Holiday during the banking crisis, the Farm Holiday Association argued that a similar holiday should be called to protect family farms.

[29] Torstenson, *Takk for Alt*, 36.

[30] This was actually higher than the going rate, likely because Joel's father negotiated on his behalf.

[31] Torstenson, *Takk for Alt*, 32.

[32] Torstenson, *Takk for Alt*, 32–33.

[33] Lawrence Quanbeck, ed., *Augsburgian of Nineteen Hundred Thirty-Nine*, *Augsburgian* Vol. 12 (Minneapolis, MN: Augsburg College and Seminary, 1939), 21, https://archives.augsburg.edu/islandora/object/AUGrepository%3A9917#page/1/mode/2up.

[34] Torstenson, *Takk for Alt*, 39.

[35] See Chapter 7, "The Heart of My Life" in *Takk for Alt: A Life Story* for a beautiful tribute to Joel's love for Fran, his wife.

[36] Jane Addams, one of the founders of American sociology, also was a founding member of FOR.

[37] Torstenson, *Takk for Alt*, 47.

[38] It is easy to imagine that his experiences on Bass Lake Farm may have contributed to the formation of the Crisis Colonies, described below.

[39] Torstenson, *Takk for Alt*, 48–53.

[40] Torstenson, *Takk for Alt*, 54.

[41] Ella Baker, "The Black Woman in the Civil Rights Struggle," speech given at the Institute of the Black World, Atlanta, Georgia, 1969, https://awpc.cattcenter.iastate.edu/2019/08/09/the-black-woman-in-the-civil-rights-struggle-1969/.

[42] Torstenson, *Takk for Alt*, 55–56.

[43] Torstenson, *Takk for Alt*, 56.

[44] Chrislock, *From Fjord to Freeway*, 210.

[45] Torstenson, *Takk for Alt*, 66.

[46] Chrislock, *From Fjord to Freeway*, 233.

[47] Chrislock, *From Fjord to Freeway*, 210.

[48] Torstenson, *Takk for Alt*, 65.

[49] Adamo, *Hold Fast*, 95.

[50] Adamo, *Hold Fast*, 47.

[51] Adamo, *Hold Fast*, 48.

[52] For a more comprehensive list of the scholars Torstenson referenced for his sabbatical work, see Joel S. Torstenson, "The Liberal Arts College in the Modern Metropolis."

[53] Joel S. Torstenson, "The Liberal Arts College in the Modern Metropolis."

[54] Paul Pribbenow, "Lessons on Vocation and Location: The Saga of Augsburg College as Urban Settlement," *Word & World* 34, No. 2 (Spring 2014): 153.

[55] See "Constant Transformation" section of this chapter.

[56] Joel S. Torstenson, *The Liberal Arts College in the Modern Metropolis.*

[57] The following includes the first sentence of each recommendation. Please see Joel S. Torstenson, *The Liberal Arts College in the Modern Metropolis*, 1976, 19–23, for the full recommendations.

[58] Moving forward in this book, the Metro-Urban Studies program will be referred to as the Urban Studies Program, regardless of time frame.

[59] "Academic Blueprint for Augsburg College", unpublished document, Augsburg University Archives, 1970.

[60] Torstenson, *Takk for Alt*, 63.

[61] Lyndon B. Johnson, "Special Message to the Congress on Urban Problems: 'The Crisis of the Cities," The American Presidency Project, accessed August 22, 2022, https://www.presidency.ucsb.edu/documents/special-message-the-congress-urban-problems-the-crisis-the-cities.

[62] See Rashad Shabazz, "Minneapolis' 'long, hot summer' of '67 – and the parallels to today's protests over police brutality," The Conversation, June 5, 2020, https://theconversation.com/minneapolis-long-hot-summer-of-67-and-the-parallels-to-todays-protests-over-police-brutality-139814, for a comparison between the events in Minneapolis in the summers of 1967 and

2020.

[63] Torstenson, *Takk for Alt*, 70.

[64] For more details about "One Day in May," (May 15, 1968) including articles, photos, and audio recordings, see "One Day in May," Augsburg University, accessed July 31, 2023, https://sites.augsburg.edu/one-day-in-may/.

[65] Joel Torstenson, "The Church Related College in the City" (paper presented at the American Lutheran College Faculties Conference at Augsburg College, Minneapolis, Minnesota, October 3, 1974). See Chapter 2 for full text.

[66] John Weirick, "On the Spot: Hana Dinku," Augsburg University, accessed August 22, 2022, https://www.augsburg.edu/now/2020/08/28/on-the-spot-6/.

[67] Torstenson, "The Church Related College."

[68] See Chapter 2.

[69] Ewald "Joe" Bash, A Rationale for the Crisis Colony Approach to Education," Unpublished Paper, 1969, Augsburg University Archives. Urban Studies Department Records.

[70] Garry Hesser, "On the Shoulders of Giants: Building on a Tradition of Experiential Education at Augsburg College" in Edward Zlotkowski (ed.), *Successful Service-Learning Programs: New Models of Excellence in Higher Education* (Anker Publishing: Bolton, MA, 1989), 19.

[71] In another Augsburg connection to HECUA, Professor Garry Hesser served on the board for over thirty years, including six years as President and four years as Vice President. When HECUA was on the verge of closing due to financial constraints, Professor Hesser served as an unpaid interim Executive Director (1992–1993) so the organization could regain finan-

cial stability. Unfortunately, multi-year travel restrictions due to the COVID-19 pandemic led to a financial crisis that could not be fixed by an unpaid Executive Director. After a fifty-year run, HECUA ceased operations in December 2021. In another demonstration of our commitment to the Torstenson legacy and the value of HECUA, Augsburg University's Center for Global Excellence and Experience took on the Conflict, Peace, and Transition in Northern Ireland Program on August 1, 2022 administered by HECUA for twenty years.

[72] Bash, "A Rationale," 18.

[73] Bash, "A Rationale," 94.

[74] Torstenson, *Takk for Alt*, 99.

[75] Chapter 3 demonstrates how Professor Garry Hesser, Torstenson's handpicked successor, was able to bring national attention to Augsburg.

REFERENCES

"Academic Blueprint for Augsburg College, 1970." Unpublished document. Augsburg University Archives.

Adamo, Phillip C. *Hold Fast to What is Good: A History of Augsburg University in 10 Objects*. Minneapolis, MN: Split Infinitive Books, 2019.

Augsburg University. "One Day in May." Accessed July 31, 2023, https://sites.augsburg.edu/one-day-in-may/.

Baker, Ella. "The Black Woman in the Civil Rights Struggle." Speech given at the Institute of the Black World, Atlanta, Georgia, 1969. Accessed July 31, 2023. https://awpc.cattcenter.iastate.edu/2019/08/09/the-black-woman-in-the-civil-rights-struggle-1969/.

Bash, Ewald "Joe." "A Rationale for the Crisis Colony Approach to Education." Unpublished Paper. Augsburg University Archives. Urban Studies Department Records, 1969.

Buffalohead, Eric. "Augsburg University Land Acknowledgement: A Case For More Than Mere Words." Unpublished manuscript. Augsburg University, 2023, 1969.

Chrislock, Carl H. *From Fjord to Freeway.* Minneapolis: Augsburg College, 1969.

Christensen, Bernhard. "The Idea of *The Lutheran Free Church.*" In *The Lutheran Free Church,* edited by Eugene L. Fevold, 316–330. Minneapolis: Augsburg Publishing House, 1969.

Hesser, Garry. "On the Shoulders of Giants: Building on a Tradition of Experiential Education at Augsburg College." In *Successful Service-Learning Programs: New Models of Excellence in Higher Education* edited by Edward Zlotkowski, 15–39. Anker Publishing: Bolton, MA, 1989.

"History." Association of Free Lutheran Congregations. Accessed August 22, 2022. https://www.aflc.org/about-us/history-of-the-aflc/.

Johnson, Lyndon B. "Special Message to the Congress on Urban Problems: 'The Crisis of the Cities'." The American Presidency Project. Accessed August 22, 2022. https://www.presidency.ucsb.edu/documents/special-message-the-congress-urban-problems-the-crisis-the-cities.

"Lutheran Free Church. 1897-1963." St. Olaf College. Accessed August 22, 2022. https://pages.stolaf.edu/locluth/lutheran-free-church/.

Pribbenow, Paul. "Lessons on Vocation and Location: The Saga of Augsburg College as Urban Settlement." *Word & World* 34, No. 2 (Spring 2014): 149–159.

Quanbeck, Lawrence, editor. *Augsburgian of Nineteen Hundred Thirty-Nine. Augsburgian* Vol. 12. Minneapolis, MN: Augsburg College and Seminary, 1939. https://archives.augsburg.edu/islandora/object/AUGrepository%3A9917#page/1/mode/2up.

Shabazz, Rashad. "Minneapolis' 'long, hot summer' of '67 – and the parallels to today's protests over police brutality." The Conversation, June 5, 2020. https://theconversation.com/

minneapolis-long-hot-summer-of-67-and-the-parallels-to-Todays-protests-over-police-brutality-139814.

Torstenson, Joel S. *Takk for Alt: A Life Story.* Minneapolis: Self Published, 2004.

Torstenson, Joel S. "The Church Related College in the City." Paper presented at the American Lutheran College Faculties Conference at Augsburg College, Minneapolis, Minnesota, October 3, 1974.

Torstenson, Joel S. *"The Liberal Arts College in the Modern Metropolis"*. Unpublished position paper presented to the faculty of Augsburg College, 1967.

Weirick, John. "On the Spot: Hana Dinku." Augsburg University. Accessed August 22, 2022. https://www.augsburg.edu/now/2020/08/28/on-the-spot-6/.

Youth.gov. "Service Learning." Accessed January 13, 2023. https://youth.gov/youth-topics/civic-engagement-and-volunteering/service-learning.

CHAPTER 2

Reprint Of "The Church-Related

College In The City"*

The Church Related College In The City[1]
Joel S. Torstenson
Professor Of Sociology And Director Of
Metro-Urban Studies
Augsburg College, Minneapolis, Minnesota

When a few months ago I was asked by David Gimsrud if I would be interested in speaking to this conference on "The Church Related College In the City" I believe that I was almost enthusiastic in my affirmative response; Not because I believed the assignment would be easy or that I thought I possessed the special competency and understanding needed—but because I intuitively felt that such a topic deserved a serious consideration at a conference such as this and that some of the recent experiences we have had at Augsburg College ought to be shared with our colleagues from other Lutheran institutions of higher learning.

* This chapter is a reprint of Joel Torstenson's essay, "The Church Related College in the City," which he presented at the American Lutheran College Faculties Conference at Augsburg College, Minneapolis, Minnesota, on October 3, 1974. In it, he expands upon the themes and ideas he first presented to Augsburg faculty in his paper, *"The Liberal Arts College in the Modern Metropolis,"* eight years earlier. In addition to presenting the philosophical underpinnings of what it means for the university to be in the city, the conference paper provides a retrospect on the innovations in teaching and learning generated by Torstenson's pedagogical approach in his own time and to the present day.

My response was also influenced, no doubt, because of my own particular involvements in a church related college's encounter with the city. For more than a quarter of a century I have been involved in these contemporary relationships of urban America. In my doctoral studies in Sociology much of my attention was focused upon the interactive relationships between changing society and its constituent institutions. In my role as professor at Augsburg, I consciously sought to promote the development of a major in sociology which would be creatively related to the social contexts of an "exploding" modern metropolis. The complexities of this task prompted me to devote my 1965–6 sabbatical to a more systematic study of higher education and urban affairs. I visited many leading cities and centers of higher learning that were developing new programs of urban emphasis. Out of these inquiries, I wrote a paper on "The Liberal Arts College in the Modern Metropolis." Since that time I have continued to be involved in Augsburg's developing urban programs. During all these years I have been a resident of Minneapolis and participated fairly actively in church and community affairs; such as being chairman of the Joint Committee for Equal Opportunity, a member of the Mayor's Commission of Human Relations, secretary for Greater Minneapolis Council of Churches Human Rights Committee, and a member of the Minneapolis Welfare Board.

From these and other academic and community experiences I have learned something about the relevance of both the cognitive and experiential dimensions of knowing and perceiving college community relations in a metro-urban world.

In addition to explaining my interest in this conference, I hope that these fragments from my "social map" may serve to inform the meanings and motifs of this paper.

THE SOCIO-CULTURAL CONTEXT

It is impossible to speak meaningfully about "the church related college in the contemporary city" without first saying something about the socio-cultural situation that gave birth to a nation-wide concern for the role of higher education in urban affairs. The most obvious consideration is of course the urban crisis. On February 28, 1968, in a message to Congress, President Lyndon Johnson made the following observation:

> Today American cities are in crisis. This clear and urgent warning rises from the decay of the decades—and is amplified from the harsh realities of the present.

As the Carnegie Commission on Higher Education noted, few would take issue with this assessment.[2] The major dimensions of the crisis are too well known by an audience such as his to warrant an extensive elaboration here. But it is important to emphasize that urban colleges and universities through-out America have come under sharp criticism for their alleged failure to respond to the challenges of the cities. Some of the sharpest criticisms have come from within academia. One of the most poignant criticisms appeared in a paper delivered by Paul W. Eberman, Dean of the College of Education at Temple University at the 23rd National Conference on Higher Education sponsored by the American Association for Higher Education in March of 1968. He opened his remarks with the following observation:

> I feel compelled to begin with the flat statement that all or most urban institutions of higher learning, including their respective colleges of education, have failed to relate themselves in meaningful and constructive ways to the urban communities which contain them– and, in particular, to that portion of the urban context which has been variously designated as the inner city, deprived, culturally disadvantaged and the like. Rather, the urban institution has been in the community in the geographic sense, but not of the community as a concerned participant in the identification and solution of critical community problems.[3]

While the central city is usually seen as the primary locus of the urban crisis, its travail and trauma cannot be fully understood apart from the relationships between the central cities and the larger metropolitan areas which have grown up around them. As the Carnegie Commission Report affirms, it is the interaction between the central city and the suburban ring that "has given rise to the sharpest manifestations of what we now call urban problems."[4] The central city's erosion of its tax base by the movement of businesses and people of high- and middle-income families to suburban areas, coupled with a simultaneous concentration of poor and minority families within the central city, have created desperate conditions for many of America's central cities. And there can be no relief from these difficulties apart from a metropolitan-regional approach to problem solving. Such an approach, however, runs contrary to pervasive historic values of local autonomy, and encounters the stubborn resistance of the multiple web of political units and districts that "balkanize" virtually every metropolitan region in the country. As Gibson Winter has so cogently stated two fundamentally conflicting principles of social organization have been at work in the birth of the metropolis: one, the principle of interdependence which has woven industries, jobs, services and other techno-economic activities into a complex web of relationships typical of community, and two, the principle of communal insulation has developed a pattern of segregated residential communities of personal associations and exclusiveness based on social, racial, ethnic, or religious similarities which seem to fragment and polarize the metropolis.[5]

Donald Canty has elaborated similar and other critical problems of the modern metropolis in the following language:

It is a profligate society, wasteful of its resources, which must someday pay the price. It is a malfunctioning society. The quality of public services declines even as local taxes continue to rise ... It is a divided society, by class and race. This has been the price of exclusivity. The new pattern of metropolis is a pattern of de facto apartheid... The new pattern of metropolis has moved us toward being an unjust society. It is deeply implicated in all of the forms of injustice wrought by poverty and racism.[6]

Whether one focuses upon the acute problems of the central cities or the pervasive long-range challenges of the incongruous metropolis, the issues raised have pertinent implications for virtually every aspect of higher learning.

HIGHER EDUCATION'S RESPONSE

But our institutions of higher learning were not well prepared to respond very creatively to these challenges. As has already been alluded to, most American colleges and universities had been nurtured in the pervasive "anti-city" ethos of American culture. Following the Oxford and Cambridge way of deliberately establishing themselves outside of the urban context that had originally provided the setting for the rise of the universities, they typically chose rural settings for their educational ventures. In the founding of Harvard, for example, rural Cambridge was chosen to escape the "moral rot" of Boston. And as the population moved westward other colleges and universities acted similarly. The University of Michigan, for example, was located in Ann Harbor, then far from the city of Detroit. Seven other universities in the "Big Ten" were also located in small cities. Even some of the universities we now consider totally urban have a history of efforts to escape the spread of the city; such as Columbia, the University of Pennsylvania, and Johns Hopkins and, as Morton and Lucia White have so systematically documented, this geographical aloofness from the city was accompanied by a pervasive anti-city orientation on the part of the intellectuals themselves.[7]

In recent years, however, and particularly after the massive outbreak of violence in our cities in the 1960s, colleges and universities were increasingly troubled by their alienation from the social realities of the modern urban world. As would be expected, universities that found themselves in the center of the troubled cities were the first to reexamine their relationships and their consciousness vis a vis the metropolis. Some of them were in deep distress about their own predicaments resulting from the urban decay that was enveloping them, such as the University of Chicago, the University of Pittsburgh, the University of Pennsylvania, Western Reserve, and Columbia, to name a few. As early as 1945, Chancellor Hutchins of the University of Chicago observed:

For the last fifteen years the university neighborhood has steadily deteriorated until today, I am ashamed to say, the university has the unfortunate distinction of having the worst housed faculty in the United States.[8]

He might well have mused about the cosmic justice that should have brought this plight to that particular university that had distinguished itself by its urban studies for decades.

Beyond their institutional predicament, it must also be emphasized that these urban universities began to seriously rethink their whole system of town-gown relationship in the context of the 20th century urban situation. Traditional patterns of teaching and research were questioned for their lack of contextual congruence with the "real world." Furthermore, their historic posture of corporate aloofness from these enveloping communities appeared increasingly indefensible. New patterns of town-gown relationships in grappling with urban problems were established: In urban research, in innovative programs of urban education, social welfare, in corrections, and in health care—to mention but a few. Perhaps the most innovative of all were the new interinstitutional and community partnerships established for urban renewal itself. Section 112 of the Housing Act of 1949 provided the legal structure and financial possibilities for this development. The University of Chicago's involvement in the Hyde Park-Kenwood developments, Western Reserve and Case Technical Institute's leadership of the "University Circle"' program in Cleveland, Columbia University's leadership in Morningside Heights of New York, and the University of Pennsylvania's role in the West Philadelphia Corporation are notable examples of the new patterns of complex town-gown relationships that were developing around the delicate and troublesome problem of renewing and/or rebuilding our central cities. All of these developments reflect a changing urban consciousness. The city was affirmed as a positive good. Higher education in all its aspects could be enriched by a conscious orientation to its multifaceted urban contexts. The new orientation was accompanied by innovative programs of urban research and education as well as by new corporate structures and procedures for relating academia to urban community systems. The spirit and character of these new developments are clearly reflected in the promotional literature of the new structures that developed. One of the annual reports of the West Philadelphia Corporation, for example, opens with the following quotation from Victor Hugo: "Nothing else in the world...not all the armies...is so powerful...as an idea whose time has come."[9]

The virtual explosion of new urban programs in colleges and universities during the last decade suggests that a transformation of the relationship between higher education and urban affairs is indeed "an idea whose time has come." We can only name some evidences of these developments here:

1. The proliferation of undergraduate urban studies programs in the United States. A 1972 inventory describes 74 such programs and lists 60 other universities and colleges considering similar programs.[10]
2. A similar proliferation of post graduate programs in urban studies.
3. A comparable development of urban research centers. A 1971-72 directory lists 217 such centers.[11]
4. An increase in the number as well as substantial changes in the character of post graduate programs in urban planning and community development.
5. A phenomenal expansion of the literature on higher education and urban affairs, including books, periodicals, and special reports. A relatively new publication by the Council of Planning Librarians provides a good illustration.[12]
6. A growing interest and activity in comparative urban studies on an international level.

AUGSBURG'S RESPONSE TO THE CITY

It was inevitable that Augsburg College should be influenced by the socio-cultural contexts that I have described. Located in the heart of one of the core cities of the Twin Cities Metropolitan Area and at the very center of that developing metropolis, it would have been virtually impossible for the College to insulate itself from such influences, even if it should have made that its conscious policy.

TOWARDS AN URBAN CONSCIOUSNESS

While there were moments of vacillation in Augsburg's history vis a vis its orientation to its developing urban environment—and certainly long intermittent periods of relative neglect in its hundred years in the city—the college did not develop an official anti-city posture. On the contrary, it had deliberately chosen the city as an advantageous location for the pursuit of its goals; and at various stages in its developments, it sought to relate creatively to the city's developments–such as in the development of its public schools, libraries, parks, and various aspects of the fine arts.

In a recent history of Augsburg, appropriately entitled *From Fjord to Freeway*, Dr. Chrislock documents some of these responses to the city.[13] He notes that the tradition established by the 19th century religious awakening in Norway which served as Augsburg's most significant guideline, had underscored the civic responsibilities of committed Christians which called for full involvement in community life. The vitality and consistency of this relationship to community were at times tested. Perhaps the most serious test came when organized efforts were made by some to have the College move out of Minneapolis and locate in the outskirts of the city. In May, 1912, the typical arguments were presented. The deterioration of the college's immediate neighborhood was lamented and the need for "more room and fresh air" was emphasized. It was noted that the old neighbors, who were supporters of the school, had already moved out to "more desirable locations" and their place had been taken by "a more or less undesirable class of people of varied race and color." Chrislock observes that this parochial view "correctly represented Augsburg's self-image in 1922."[14] It was not until 1946 that this lure of the suburbs was put at rest by a unanimous vote of the board of trustees committing the college to a long-range campus expansion within its historic inner city location.[15]

While the rationale for this commitment no doubt involved several considerations, there is good reason to believe that by this time under the leadership of President Bernhard Christensen "education for service" had come to have special positive meaning for Augsburg's relationship to the city of Minneapolis. Christensen's leadership was not only reflected in his words of encouragement of faculty and students to become involved in church and community affairs. He assumed many significant responsibilities on his own. Of particular relevance to this paper was his role on Mayor Hubert H. Humphrey's Council of Human Relations, created in 1946 to work against racial and religious discrimination in all areas of Minneapolis life. As chairman of that council from 1948 to 1950 and as an active member two years thereafter he contributed much to Augsburg's sensitivity to one of the most critical issues of American urban life and also provided a model for college-community relationships in other contexts as well. Both students and faculty sensed that their interest in and concern for the quality of life in the city had the unequivocal and sustained moral support of the President of the College.

When the so-called "urban crisis" came, this positive support for "community service and good human relations" had left its mark upon both the College's curriculum as well as its general orientation as a college in the city. During the turbulent sixties, with the vigorous support of its new president, Oscar Anderson, the College articulated this orientation more explicitly and developed new programs to implement its emerging metro-urban consciousness.

By the end of the sixties, this consciousness had been both publicly affirmed and internally adopted as one of the official policies of the College. When, in 1969, the College celebrated its hundredth anniversary, it organized its centennial symposium around the theme "The Challenge of the City." This historic event provided a strategic occasion for publicly affirming the college's developing urban thrust. In the same year, President Anderson wrote in *Augsburg College Now* about the metropolis as the "unlimited laboratory" affirming the educational uses of the city, and the idea of the college's partnership with it, as an expansion of its educational role. Internally, this orientation had worked its way into the Academic Blueprint for Augsburg College which had emerged out of long and comprehensive institutional self-study and had been officially approved by the faculty and Board of Regents as the academic agenda for the 1970's. The following statement from that Blueprint was identified as one of the four basic presuppositions guiding the College's future development:

> Augsburg College should develop the greatest educational benefit from its urban location and should contribute to the enrichment of the life of the city. The College recognizes that the city is simultaneously a most important educational resource, an appropriate context for the College's participation in the life of the community, and itself, a most timely object of study. However, the College must not forget that it is a bearer and preserver of the tradition of humane studies; as such it should continue to be a distinct educational community within the city even as it directs some of its energies to tile needs of the city.[16]

AN EXPERIMENT IN NEW FORMS AND STRATEGIES

As these new attitudes toward the city and towards urban oriented liberal learning were developing, many new "urban programs" were initiated and tested. One of the first was an experiment in metro-urban communication known as the "Town Meeting of the Twin Cities." It was one of the first educational ventures in Minnesota that was financed under Title One of the Higher Education Act of 1965. Consistent with the goals of that act, the program was interinstitutional in auspices, and community-oriented in its purposes and concerns. The Board of College

Education of the A.L.C., Augsburg Colleges and KTCA-TV were the chief sponsors; but a vast network of churches, schools, social agencies, adult educational organizations, etc., became significant participants in the venture.

It was perhaps the first concerted, cooperative venture between the college and its sponsoring church in articulating their common concern for the city. And of course it made Augsburg's emerging urban orientation visible to many new audiences in its Midwest metropolis.

AUGSBURG'S RESPONSE TO THE URBAN CRISIS

"When the time for burning" came to Minneapolis, a new spirit of urgency was introduced. On March 27, 1968, following a luncheon with Andrew Hatcher, former Associate Press Secretary for President John F. Kennedy, President Anderson called an impromptu meeting of several faculty members present to discuss how the college might best respond to the urban crisis. Out of this meeting came the idea of "A Day in May" when the whole college community would listen to the voices of despair and revolt from the inner cities of Minneapolis and St. Paul. The impact of that dramatic experience of students and faculty learning directly from its surrounding community about some of the deeply felt feelings of frustration and anger of hurting people in our cities was intense. Educational "business as usual" seemed no longer defensible. Something had to be done! A couple of days later President Anderson received a letter from Dr. Loren Halvorson from the Board of College Education which set in motion a program of response to the urban crisis. It laid out a preliminary design for an Augsburg "Center of Urban Care" to be funded for two years by the American Lutheran Church. By the fall of that year (1969) the Reverend William Youngdahl, known for his *Time for Burning* film, was on the scene directing the affairs of such a center.

The special competencies and particular personal passions of Bill Youngdahl were strategically important for Augsburg in this period of inner city turbulence. He became an important link between the College and the various sub-communities that had become deeply involved in the ongoing urban crisis. He served as a member of the Communications Task Force of the Minneapolis Urban Coalition and represented the College President at such meetings of the Board of Directors of that Coalition that the President was unable to attend. He was a member of the Minneapolis Commission on Human Relations and gave that body sensitive and creative leadership. He was involved as a speaker and consultant to a great many civic and religious groups in our metropolitan area. Internally, he worked with students and faculty and administrative leaders in developing new college responses to the challenges of minority education. A new program called FAME (Fund for Assistance to Minority Education) was created, and several new courses in Black Studies were initiated. Special linkages were established between the college and "The Way"—a Black community center that had emerged in North Side Minneapolis following the riots in 1967. In cooperation with Antioch College in Ohio, some of the leaders of that organization created "The Way University." Some of Augsburg's "Black Studies" courses were cooperative ventures between The Way University and Augsburg College. Augsburg's Dean, Dr. Kenneth Bailey, is a member of the Board of "The Way University" and linkages between the two institutions continue.

North Minneapolis also became the locus of another innovative educational venture in the summer of 1968—"The Crisis Colony." It was an experiment with a "live-in" learning program in which students from various A.L.C. Colleges shared in the life and work of a ghetto community while studying the nature and dynamics of modern urban life for college credit. Major leadership in this experiment came from the Reverend Ewald Bash from the Youth Office of the American Lutheran Church. Students registered for the program through Augsburg College. Dr. Myles Stenshoel and Dr. Joel S. Torstenson of Augsburg College were faculty participants in the program. Ghetto "street people," indigenous leaders of local community organizations and civil rights leaders were hired as "adjunct professors." Each student was engaged in volunteer work in strategic agencies, organizations, or situations which would provide a sensitive "participant-observer" situation.

The rationale for the Crisis Colony was not only related to the Urban Crisis, but was rather a response to a larger "societal crisis" and the "educational crisis" related to it. As "Joe" Bash put it, the "Crisis Colony" experiment emerged out of "new understandings of the university's relation to society."[17] No longer was objectivity alone an adequate approach to learning, he emphasized. Teaching and learning must happen in dynamics of experiential encounter.

The Crisis Colony was continued in the following year for a second "semester in the city." Living in the third floor of what was once a Jewish Synagogue and participating actively in a Minneapolis political campaign, the students experienced what it meant to encounter the wrath of city political leaders who regarded their activities as inimical to their best interests. They learned firsthand (experientially) about politics and power in an inner city community.

This "Crisis Colony" program has since become the Metropolitan Urban Studies Term (MUST) of the Higher Education Consortium for Urban Affairs, of which more will be said later.

THE CONSERVATION OF HUMAN RESOURCES PROGRAM

Another educational strategy for articulating higher education with the community that was initiated at this time was a new "co-learning model" of education. A brief description of the first experiment provides its best explanation. In the fall of 1969, a course in "Crime and Society" was staged in Stillwater Prison. The class was made up of 17 Augsburg students, 11 prison inmates, and 4 correctional officers. All read the same basic readings. In this sense it was a traditional college course. But the class situation was substantially altered. All students became teachers as well as learners of and from each other. The instructor, Professor Cal Appleby, put a main emphasis upon his role as an enabler for learning, rather than a "giver of Knowledge" in the area. (Incidentally, it is appropriate to emphasize that Professor Appleby was the guiding spirit in the development of this program.) Role playing, role reversals, etc., became important stratagems in learning about the culture and dynamics of crime and criminal justice in contemporary America. The student reaction to this experiment—both of the prison inmates and the college students—was enthusiastic. The following year other college courses from several disciplines were similarly taught at Stillwater. Substantial funding support from the Governor's Crime Commission in 1971 has helped expand the program at both Stillwater and such other correctional institutions as the Women's Prison at Shakopee and the St. Cloud Reformatory. Some of the inmate students, since paroled, have become full time "free" students continuing their liberal learning in various colleges. A similar program was developed in two metropolitan mental hospitals where college students joined selected hospital patients and staff personnel for the study of "Mental Health and the Social Order." In the following year (1970–1971) the program was introduced at Trevilla of Robbinsdale, a rehabilitation center for the physically handicapped. Here too people formerly deprived from college education have now been given such opportunity.

This innovative strategy of college extension into the community has now become an integral part of Augsburg's educational program and is being directed by a special studies structure known as the C.H.R. (Conservation of Human Resources). Further details of this program will be described at another session of this Conference.

AUGSBURG'S SOCIAL SCIENCE RESEARCH CENTER

During the 1960s Augsburg's Department of Sociology became involved in the management and direction of several Twin City Community studies. The experience gained from these studies led to the creation of the Social Science Research Center with a full-time faculty director, Dr. Robert Clyde. The following brief digest of some of its developing activities indicated its expanding involvement in Urban Affairs:

1. Metro-Urban Community Studies
    a. Campus Areas in Midwest Metropolis, 1964.
    b. Phalen Park: An Urban Community in a Midwest Metropolis, 1965.
    c. A Profile and Prospectus of Summit University: An Inner City Community, 1966
    d. The North End Community, 1967.
2. Leadership in obtaining Title I funding for an intercollege, interdisciplinary analysis and assessment of the Minneapolis Model City experiment. The director of The Research Center guided the research done by faculty members of the various colleges making up the Higher Education Consortium for Urban Affairs.
3. Direction and Administration of an Inter-Institutional, interdisciplinary ecumenical Young Family Studies Program.
4. Social Area Analysis for the Federally Funded "Experimental Schools Project" in Southeast Minneapolis.
5. Evaluation of a "Black Voices Television Series" supported by KTCA-TV.
6. Development of a white racism scale and the application of it in various social situations involving sensitivity testing and training.
7. Current involvement in a new program of "social cost accounting" of leading metropolitan corporations.

AUGSBURG'S METRO–URBAN STUDIES PROGRAM

All the above-mentioned developments inevitably influenced thinking about their relationships to the overall educational program of the College. Were they to be perceived as special programs on the edge of Augsburg's principal tasks; or were they somehow to be integrally related to the development of an entire college approach to higher education in the context of a metro-urban world? If the first option was chosen, the logic might have led to the creation of a separate Augsburg center for urban affairs, as has been done in several institutions of higher learning. This option was considered and rejected. Instead, it was assumed that all of liberal learning had meaning for an urban world and that liberal arts in the 20th century becomes fundamentally education in the urban arts. The College's challenge was to see to it that its liberal arts program would be made more congruous with realities of the world about it. Out of this orientation the following recommendation for curricular development was written into the Academic Blueprint for Augsburg College in 1970:

> During the early part of the next decade, Augsburg College should develop a more extensive and coordinated program of urban studies. The program which is already under way should include an interdisciplinary major and minor in Urban Studies.[18]

To implement this recommendation, a student-faculty committee was created for the purpose of preparing a proposed Metro-Urban Studies Program. The participating faculty members represented every academic division of the College. At the outset, the committee examined urban studies programs that had been developed in other colleges and universities. A file of such programs had been started by the committee's chairman during his years as chairman of the Higher Education Consortium for Urban Affairs. Special attention was given to inter-disciplinary programs developed by liberal arts-oriented institutions, such as Columbia University, Dartmouth College, and Saint Peter's College. Out of these explorations, together with counsel given by department chairmen and other members of the faculty, the Committee established the following guidelines for its proposed program:

1. The Urban Studies program should as far as possible be integrated into Augsburg's overall educational structure and not be set apart as an addendum to it.
2. The program should reflect a creative input from every academic division of the college.
3. Systematic strategies should be developed for making maximum use of Augsburg's metro-urban environment as a learning laboratory.

4. The program should contribute to the achievement of the following objectives:
   a. An increased appreciation of the creative role of the city in modern life and culture.
   b. A keener perception of the nature of the modern metropolis as a community system.
   c. A fuller understanding of the organizational structures of modern urban life.
   d. A firmer grasp of the dynamics of urban change and its concomitant problems.
   e. A stronger motivation for responding creatively to the problems and opportunities of urban life.
   f. A greater competence in a variety of human resource skills typically required in urban living.

The Metro-Urban Studies Program, which was adopted by the college in January, 1971, included the following major components:

1. An interdisciplinary Metro-Urban Studies major made up a list of required core courses and suggested electives from various disciplines.
2. An urban studies "concentration" which could be linked with various majors in the college.
3. A general education requirement in urban concern for all students of the college.

The following list of course offerings in various departments is indicative of the interdisciplinary character of the program:

Art - Urban Environmental Esthetics
Biology - Man and the Urban Environment
Economics - Economic Issues of the Urban Environment
Education - School and Society (Special Attention to Urban Education)
English - The City in American Literature
History - European Urban History
Political Science - American Government and Politics: Metropolitan Complex
Sociology - The City and Metro-Urban Planning

Students majoring in Metro-Urban Studies are required to take a core program in research and have at least one course of community-based internship or independent study. The opportunities for an urban internship have been improved during the last two years by the establishment of a college-wide Metro-Urban Studies Internship Program (MUSIP).

Other programs have been developing out of the various academic departments for making strategic use of the city as a learning laboratory, such as a new major in human services, systematically articulating social work theory and field experience in a wide variety of agencies and organizations of the city; expanded and innovative uses of the metro-urban school situations for the teaching of teachers in the department of education; the development of a new program in geriatric social service worked out in cooperation with the appropriate agencies and organizations in the area; the development of new recreation leadership programs of great importance to inner city youth, etc.

The pervading motif in these developments is the perception of the metropolis as a laboratory of educational resources. The challenge has been to identify these resources and to develop structural strategies for their effective use. One of the latest developments of such strategies has been the initiation of a "Professor of the City" program, funded by the Hill Family Foundation, which makes possible the use of specially talented persons from the larger community in strategic courses designed to add new dimensions to the curriculum.

INTER-COLLEGE PARTNERSHIPS IN URBAN AFFAIRS

As the College's involvements in new urban relationships and programs grew, the more acute became its awareness of the complexities and the need for cooperative partnerships with other colleges and institutions of higher learning, sharing similar concerns. One of the organizations that emerged out of this need was the Higher Education Consortium for Urban Affairs (HECUA). The initiative for the development of this organization came from Dean Bailey of Augsburg College in the summer of 1968 in the hopes of exploring the possibility of inter-college sponsorship of such experimental learning programs as the "Crisis Colony." By the fall of that year enough colleges had become involved in the emerging organization to assume joint sponsorship of the "Crisis Colony" which had now moved to the Model City Neighborhood in South Minneapolis. The following year the organization was legally incorporated as the Higher Education Consortium for Urban Affairs. The five goals of the corporation were: 1) develop urban-related curricula for students by establishing and operating inter-institutional programs and by assisting member colleges in planning their own programs; 2) collect, discuss and disseminate information about the programs, resources, and need of the member colleges; 3) provide structures and procedures for institutional participation in programs which might be developed in cooperation with urban organizations; 4) identify research needs, resources and interests, and encourage inter-institutional research in urban affairs; 5) develop other programs consistent with the interests and resources of the member institutions and urban communities as the consortium deems useful.

The following is a list of some of the major programs developed by this Consortium so far:

1. The continued sponsorship of the Metropolitan Urban Studies Term (formerly the Crisis Colony) located in the Model Neighborhood of Minneapolis.
2. "An Urban Planning and Community Development" seminar which brought together 10 college students and 10 resident planners of the Model City for an examination of inner city planning with maximum citizen participation. This was partially funded by a Title I grant and operated for two terms in 1971-72.
3. A course in Criminology called "Issues in the Reform of the Criminal Justice System," jointly sponsored by HECUA and the Correctional Service Association of Minnesota, and taught by the Commissioner of Corrections of that state. In the first two semesters that this course was taught, 80 students from eight

member colleges participated.

4. The development of the Scandinavian Urban Studies Term (SUST) jointly sponsored by the Consortium and the University of Oslo's International Summer School. The program was begun in the fall of 1973 under the direction of Joel S. Torstenson of Augsburg College and is continuing in the fall of 1974 under the direction of James Brother of St. Olaf College. Plans are already under way for continuing the program in the fall of 1975.

5. A Conference on "Urbanization and Higher Education" at Macalester College in 1972.

6. Acted as fiscal agent for a Bremer Foundation funded scholarship program for ex-offenders at MECUA member colleges.

7. A research venture analyzing and evaluating the Model Cities program in Minneapolis. This venture too was funded in part by Title I funds of the Higher Education Act.

The following institutions were listed as members of the Consortium in the spring of 1974: Augsburg College, Augustana College, Bethel College, Carleton College, College of St. Catherine, College of St. Thomas, Macalester College, St. Olaf College, and the University of Minnesota through its Center for Urban and Regional Affairs.

Last year Augsburg became a participant in another inter-college partnership for urban affairs which emerged as part of the new cooperative "Take-Five" Program between Hamline University, College of St. Catherine, College of St. Thomas, Macalester College, and Augsburg. Major attention so far has been focused upon teacher education in inner city schools and the development of cooperative urban library resources.

AUGSBURG AND URBAN RENEWAL: THE ROLE OF THE COLLEGE AS A CORPORATE CITIZEN OF THE METROPOLIS

In the preceding section of the paper I have reviewed the development of changing orientation to historic town-gown relations and described its impact upon the changing roles of the college as "educator," "researcher," and to some extent, "community service agents" in the context of its changing urban environment. But the picture of this changing college in the changing city would be incomplete without a sketch of its changing role as a corporate citizen of the metropolis. Augsburg's recent history has been replete with illustrations of virtually every kind of experience that the new literature on Higher Education and Urban Affairs describes under the rubric the "University's Role as a Corporate Citizen."

The most dramatic has been its experiences as an inescapable participant in the turbulent drama of the developments that have occurred in its immediate neighborhood, the Cedar-Riverside Area. If the college ever did enjoy the luxury of planning its own campus community with little or no concern for its impact upon its surrounding community setting, that has long since ceased to be a corporate option. Furthermore, the college could only with peril remain indifferent to the dramatic developments taking place all around it: the freeway development on its southern border; the expansion of the University of Minnesota into the Cedar-Riverside area to the north of it; the expansion of the two hospitals on the north and east; the growing obsolescence of the commercial and residential properties throughout the Cedar-Riverside Area; and the host of problems related to the socio-cultural incongruities that accompanied these developments.

Time will not allow a documentation of Augsburg's corporate role as full participant in a long and complex chapter in the Minneapolis Urban Renewal history. Suffice to say, Augsburg representatives joined those of other private corporations, neighborhood residential groups, the University of Minnesota, business institutions on Cedar Avenue, various units of local government, churches, and social work agencies in a long and complicated process of assessing the community's prospects for the future. This led eventually to the adoption of an Urban Renewal plan for the area in which such private institutions as Augsburg were given the opportunity (perhaps mandate would be more accurate) to be a participating agent in the Cedar-Riverside renewal process.

In 1971, largely through the efforts of one of Cedar-Riverside associates, the Cedar-Riverside area was designated by the Department of Housing and Urban Development as its first "New Town-In Town" in the United States; drastically altering the projected shape and composition of Augsburg's environment. Burton Fosse, Augsburg's Vice President for Finance and Management, who together with Presidents Christensen and Anderson, has been intimately and deeply involved in all these developments, indicates their meaning for Augsburg in the following observation: "Augsburg's investment in the community has been more than an investment in buildings and improvements to suit its own needs. Through its representatives, it has participated for a decade and a half in the planning, the community organizing, and the politics which set the stage for the development of a new community."[19]

Since this is a Lutheran Faculties Conference, it is appropriate to note that a similar statement could be made about the role of Trinity Lutheran Congregation which has had a long history of special relationships to the college as well as to Cedar-Riverside.

During the last decade or so, this congregation has assumed important leadership responsibilities in community care and concern for this inner-city community. It has helped bring together the multiplicity of groups and institutions in the area for the purpose of finding a means of making a viable community for the future. Both the congregation and Augsburg helped prepare the way for the urban renewal decisions. Both played an important role in helping to create the University Community Development Corporation in 1965. This brought together virtually all leading institutions and social organizations in the area for joint thinking and action in community building. This is essentially a "cultural borrowing" from the West Philadelphia Corporation alluded to earlier in this paper. In recent years both Trinity and Augsburg have been active in the "West Bank Process" which brings together the private institutions and churches in the area for communication and shared deliberations and action. President Anderson of Augsburg College is chairman of this organization. Anyone familiar with the local situation knows that there can be no turning back for the college from its role as an institutional participant in these urban renewal developments. Every informed person also knows that it has been and will continue to be a difficult and delicate corporate role of decision-making in the context of deep and pervasive community conflicts.

If Augsburg's involvements in the Cedar-Riverside developments have been most immediate and pervasive, they are far from being the complete story of its role as corporate citizen in the contemporary scene. They are rather illustrative of all the new corporate linkages being established between the college and the entire web of private and public corporate systems in our time; such as the federal, state, metropolitan, and local governmental units involved in urban redevelopments, as well as such other structures as the Urban Coalition, the Model City, civil and human rights organizations, etc. The new and increased demands upon the administrative officers of the college that has accompanied these developments are formidable, and no doubt puts special strains on the limited resources of the college.

The new roles of corporate citizenship also become special challenges for the Board of Regents. New perceptions as well as new perspectives have been required of them too. In order to assist the Board in responding to these challenges, the present administration of the college has made it a policy to seek out persons with special experiences and understandings vis a vis the metro-urban world to serve as members of the Board when new members are selected.

SOME ISSUES AND ASSESSMENTS

This account of Augsburg's response to the city has of course been written from the perspective of a participant observer with a spirit of "sympathetic understanding." As I indicated at the beginning of the paper, such a perspective flows naturally from my particular social geography. I have understood that my primary task here has been to give as meaningful a picture of the complexities of the changing responses of a particular church college to the revolutionary changes taking place in the larger metro-urban world of which it is a part. Many aspects of the college's life have, of course, been overlooked, not because they are less important, but because they have not been thought to be as useful in accenting the drama of change which was being documented.

It should also be noted that in this documentation I have purposely avoided dealing with the conflicts and tensions that have inevitably accompanied the changes. There have, of course, been debates about the appropriate roles of a liberal arts college and its encounter with culture. There have, of course, been divergent views about the destiny and meaning of the modern metropolis; involving differing conclusions concerning the appropriate responses of the college to it. The tension between the "localite" and "cosmopolite" orientations to the world I'm sure has been a source of psychic struggle within, as well as between, individual members of our academic community. There have, of course, been the typical misunderstandings between the departments of the college, and presumably people in every academic discipline have been torn between their loves and loyalties toward their particular disciplines and their sense of obligation to engage in the difficult task of a "trans-disciplinary" response which seems to be demanded by the crises of contemporary times.[20] Of course, there have been controversies concerning educational philosophies; such as the controversy over experiential vs. cognitive learning, or the debate between "liberal learning" and "career-oriented" education, etc. And, of course, there have been considerable differences of opinion concerning the implications of the college's developing responses to the city for theology, and for the special responsibilities that derive from the fact that Augsburg is a church related college.

One might lament these tensions and seek to avoid them, but from my limited study of theology and my more extensive (though limited) sociological understandings, I'm persuaded that the tensions have been and will continue to be inevitable, and that they have been and continue to be creative. It is my hope that in the next few years the college will be allowed a bit more serenity, so that it can reflect more deeply about the issues that have surfaced, sift out the changes that have been the most important and constructive, and find appropriate ways of assimilating them into the life and culture of a college that has made its commitment to the metropolis an integral part of its theological faith and educational philosophy.

ENDNOTES

[1] Paper presented at the American Lutheran College Faculties Conference at Augsburg College, Minneapolis, Minnesota, October 3, 1974.

[2] Carnegie Commission on Higher Education, *The Campus and the City* (New York: McGraw-Hill Book Company, 1972), 11.

[3] Paul Eberman, "The Urban Community: Laboratory for the Preparation of Teachers for the Inner City," paper presented to a Sectional Meeting of the 23rd National Conference on Higher Education, sponsored by the American Association for Higher Education, Chicago, March 5, 1968.

[4] Carnegie Commission, *The Campus and the City*, 9–10.

[5] Gibson Winter, *The Suburban Captivity of the Churches* (New York: The MacMillan Company, 1962), 22–23.

[6] Donald Canty, "Metropolity," *City*, March–April, 1972, 29–44.

[7] William Slayton, "The University, the City, and Urban Renewal," in *The University, The City, and Urban Renewal* by Charles G. Dobbins (Washington, D. C.: American Council on

Education, 1966), 1–9; Martin J. Klotsche, *An Urban University and the Future of Our Cities* (New York: Harper and Row, 1966); Morton and Lucia White, *The Intellectual Versus the City* (Cambridge: Harvard University Press, 1961).

[8] Slayton, "The University," 4.

[9] West Philadelphia Corporation, *University City: The Fifth Annual Report of the West Philadelphia Corporation* (West Philadelphia Corporation, 1965).

[10] Henry Bischoff, *Urban Studies Now* (Jersey City: St. Peter's College, 1972).

[11] The Urban Institute, University Urban Research Center (Washington D. C., 1971).

[12] Council of Planning Librarians, *Institutions of Higher Education and Urban Problems: A Bibliography and Review for Planners, Center for Urban and Regional Studies*, University of North Carolina, Chapel Hill, 1973.

[13] Carl H. Chrislock, *From Fjord to Freeway* (Minneapolis, Augsburg College, 1969), 121–134.

[14] Chrislock, *From Fjord to Freeway*, 133.

[15] Chrislock, *From Fjord to Freeway*, 201.

[16] "Academic Blueprint for Augsburg College", unpublished document, Augsburg University Archives, 1970.

[17] Ewald "Joe" Bash. "A Rationale for the Crisis Colony Approach to Education," Unpublished Paper, 1969, Augsburg University Archives. Urban Studies Department Records.

[18] "Academic Blueprint for Augsburg College."

[19] *Augsburg College Now* (Augsburg College, 1972), 9.

[20] Elden Jacobson, "Urban Curricula and the Liberal Arts Colleges," *Liberal Education* 58 (May 1972): 295.

REFERENCES

Augsburg College Now. (Augsburg College, 1972)

Bash, Ewald "Joe." "A Rationale for the Crisis Colony Approach to Education." Unpublished Paper, Augsburg University Archives. Urban Studies Department Records, 1969.

Bischoff, Henry. *Urban Studies Now.* Jersey City: St. Peter's College, 1972.

Canty, Donald. "Metropolity." *City* (March-April, 1972): 29-44.

Carnegie Commission on Higher Education. *The Campus and the City.* New York: McGraw-Hill Book Company, 1972.

Council of Planning Librarians. *Institutions of Higher Education and Urban Problems: A Bibliography and Review for Planners.* Center for Urban and Regional Studies. Chapel Hill: University of North Carolina, 1973.

Chrislock, Carl H. *From Fjord to Freeway.* Minneapolis: Augsburg College, 1969.

Eberman, Paul. "The Urban Community: Laboratory for the Preparation of Teachers for the Inner City." A paper presented to a Sectional Meeting of the 23rd National Conference on Higher Education, sponsored by the American Association for Higher Education, Chicago, March 5, 1968.

Jacobson, Elden. *Higher Education and Urban Affairs - An Approach for Metropolitan Washington.* Washington Center for Metropolitan Studies, Washington D.C., 1969.

Jacobson, Elden. "Urban Curricula and the Liberal Arts Colleges." *Liberal Education* 58 (May 1972): 286–297.

Klotsche, J. Martin. *An Urban University and the Future of Our Cities.* New York: Harper and Row, 1966.

Slayton, William. "The University, the City, and Urban Renewal." In *The University, The City, and Urban Renewal* by Charles G. Dobbins. Washington, D.C.: American Council on Education, 1964. The Urban Institute. University Urban Research Center. Washington D.C., 1971.

Torstenson, Joel S. "The Liberal Arts College in the Modern

Metropolis." Unpublished position paper presented to the faculty of Augsburg College, 1967.

West Philadelphia Corporation. *University City: The Fifth Annual Report of the West Philadelphia Corporation*. Philadelphia, 1965.

White, Morton, and Lucia White. *The Intellectual Versus the City*. Cambridge: Harvard University Press, 1961.

Winter, Gibson. *The Suburban Captivity of the Churches*. New York: The MacMillan Company, New York, 1962.

QUESTIONS FOR FURTHER REFLECTION

1. Who are the individuals in your institution who have led efforts to link campus and wider community?
   How are these individuals honored and recognized? Who knows their stories and can tell them in this moment and in the future?

2. In Torstenson's "The Church-Related College in the City" paper, he mentioned how colleges and universities during the 1960s and 1970s came under sharp criticism for failing to respond to the challenges of cities. Are there challenges today in which your institution has shown leadership?
   Are there additional ways your institution could more directly address the issues of our time?

3. In our historical examination of Augsburg's curriculum, we see how language, practices, and pedagogies have shifted with time. What are some of the ways these things have shifted at your institution?

4. This section highlights how Augsburg has embraced the urban landscape of the Twin Cities and related opportunities. What unique opportunities are presented to institutions in suburban and rural communities?

Crisis Colony, the Origi...

PROJECT OF YOUTH DIVISION

for the Augsburg P...

The Inner City Teaches

- Visitors Collection of Indian speakers
- Barb Orfield and Inner City Art among the people
- Symptoring in city parks Art School
- Vest pocket Parks and students
- John Ylvisaker and Students with Contemporary Music
- Drama and Northside High Schoolers
- Theological Semester in the Inner City
- Motion Pictures in Inner Cities

Black Music and Developing Thee Whole / AIM Beginnings

The Way as a Developing Institution

The Way's Stand against National Guard Squad July

Other North Side Agencies and their work

North Side Churches and their Services which we conducted

30 STUDENTS FROM ALL OVER THE USA / Sojourning Students and Wayfares ALL LEARNING from city

A LEARNING COMMUNITY
Leadership and Associates (Scholato, Hayden)
Teaching Leaders Orfield, Ylvisaker
Student leaders
Joe Bash

LIVED AT PLYMOUTH YOUTH CENTER (Soon torn down)

AUGSBURG'S ENTRANCE UNDER THE LEADERSHIP OF JOEL TORSTENSON AND THE URBAN STAFF

ALL SUPPORTED BY YOUTH DIVISION (ALC) AND LUTHERAN SOCIAL SERVICE (ALC) PAUL BOE

TORSTENSON'S SABBATICAL YEAR DETERMINES
ENTRANCE INTO CITY PROBLEMS DIRECTLY
TORSTENSON AND JOE BASH JOIN FORCES
FIRST EXPERIMENT — SUMMER, 1968
At: Closing Catholic School TO BE TORN DOWN
TORSTENSON LEADS THE FRAME OF THE CITY
AND NORTH SIDE INNER CITY
EVENING LEARNING FROM COMMUNITY LEADERS
STUDENTS WITH SPECIAL PROBLEMS FROM DISCIPLINE
WORSHIP WITH YLVISAKER AT NEARBY CHURCHES
RECEIVED BY AUGSBURG WITH EDUCATIONAL STYLE, TOO.

SECOND EXPERIMENT - SPRING, 1969, 3RD QUARTER
GREAT DIFFICULTIES IN HOUSING
Early Synagogue failed after one week — one minyan of 10 was still there
Moved to synagogue neighbor, a funeral home nearby
Basement large and quite usable. Lived upstairs in a burned building! Not student-like but livable
Black Mood somber too somewhat negative
Speakers from community. Projects like "Voter Registration of the community"
Group gradually became more united behind Black Candidate, Bill Smith, though never officially (He lost)
MODERN SERVICES AT CHURCHES (Ylvisaker leads)
Sudden Command to leave premises by city Housing North Side
Group stayed! Until May 25th, our closing date! City likes!
Note Schiato experiments with whites in the suburbs
Again experiment received well. Continue ventures
but in a new support form.

THIRD EXPERIMENT, 197...
Augsburg unites with o...
of the area. Each ne...
(New forms; new fo...
Can project be transfer...
Set up in Southside Inner...
Had to renovate house for...
(they lived separately first...
Worship given up because o...
Southside had less poor b...
inquiry broader but lea...
Students turning in work,
Faculty from the commu...
Experiment continues so...
Entered "the" male chauve...
William Smith and Bryan...
After the experiments, S...
returns to national a...
Again well-received

AUGSBURG DEVEL...
Bill Youngdahl's...
Opens its own...
for Physically...
HECUA opens ov...
in Scandinavia...
CENTER FOR COM...
DEVELOPMENT OF A...
"Vocation...

FROM CRISIS COLONY TO PLACE-BASED JUSTICE: INTRODUCTION

As this book transitions to more contemporary examples, it bears repeating that all institutions of higher education, as well as individuals that make up campus communities, are undergoing constant transformation. Torstenson's paper "The Church Related College in the City" documented significant accomplishments, but also demonstrated the need for further progress. Some calls for further progress were made in the paper, while others became clear when reflecting on the social, structural, and historical context at the time of its presentation. For example, place-based justice initiatives and an institutional commitment to equity were not part of the lexicon in 1974 as they are today. Because Torstenson showed such innovative and forward-thinking thought leadership at the time, he created a path for constant change as Augsburg continues to redefine our commitments to our students and neighbors.

The following chapters highlight how the strength of Torstenson's legacy allowed for those following in his footsteps to grow as well as redefine what he started. Aided by the foundation of his work, more recent faculty, staff, and campus presidents have been able to reinforce Augsburg's commitment to being a university with the city while simultaneously working to be a more equitable institution. The combined efforts of many members of the Augsburg community, including those highlighted in the following chapters, have created a culture of pedagogical innovation, leading to accelerated structural changes within the institution. Over the last few decades, Augsburg University has built an exemplary organizational structure to promote experiential education, often harnessing the resources of Minneapolis, and becoming a national leader along the way.

CHAPTER 3

Passing The Torstenson Baton:

How a Hand-Picked Successor Put Augsburg's

Curricular Innovations in the National

Experiential Education Spotlight

Anyone with experience in higher education knows that trends come and go. Innovative ideas gather traction, are shared at academic conferences, gain the attention of faculty and administrators, and often become campus-wide initiatives. All too often, the excitement and funding for the initiatives wear off and the faculty and staff initially charged with carrying out the work begin to dwindle as they move on to newer ideas. If you are lucky enough to spend a couple of decades on a college campus, you will likely see some of the curricular innovations from early in your career once again presented as new ideas and initiatives. At Augsburg, however, experiential education was never a fleeting pedagogical fad, but an ongoing innovation that has taken effort, coordination, and dedicated leadership.

NOT A PASSING FAD

The foundation laid by Professor Joel S. Torstenson, articulated through his 1967 post-sabbatical report to the faculty, *"The Liberal Arts College in the Modern Metropolis,"* continues to ground Augsburg's focus on the city as a learning laboratory, a locus for research, and as an opportunity for community service.[1] This has not happened by chance. Because Professor Torstenson remained on the faculty for a decade after he articulated what it meant to be a liberal arts college in a metropolis, he was able to establish a model of transition that ensured Augsburg would not lose sight of the fundamental transformations he helped to create on campus. This chapter examines how Professor Torstenson's hand-picked successor, Professor Garry W. Hesser, helped to grow Augsburg University's focus on teaching and learning based on experiential learning, service-learning, the importance of place, and Augsburg's commitment to the city. Through his efforts, Professor Hesser's leadership helped to deeply embed these pedagogical commitments into Augsburg's curriculum while also shining the national spotlight on the university.

PASSING THE BATON

Throughout the late 1970s, Professor Torstenson continued to be a driving force at Augsburg, but his energy, ideas, and teaching ability were of no consideration when he reached mandatory retirement age.[2] The predictability of a hard deadline for retirement did have an advantage in that it provided time for Torstenson to prepare for his departure from Augsburg.[3] Torstenson had amassed a great deal of social capital at Augsburg, so he convinced his department and campus administrators that his successor should be hired a year before his retirement. Social capital alone, however, was not enough as it also took financial resources to cover two faculty salaries for one position. To help remedy the financial issue, one of Torstenson's colleagues, Professor Robert Grams, took an unpaid year of absence to work in personnel management for the state of Minnesota.

With a plan in order, the Department of Sociology conducted a national search in which Garry W. Hesser was chosen to carry the Torstenson baton.

Figure 3.1
Professor Garry Hesser.
Augsburg Now 67, No. 2–3
(Winter/Spring 2005).

Augsburg University
Archives. Used with
permission.

Professor Emeritus Hesser served Augsburg from 1977 to 2017 as a member of the Department of Sociology, the Urban Studies Program, and as the inaugural Martin Olav Sabo Professor of Citizenship and Democracy. The fact that Hesser, not subject to mandatory retirement, was on the faculty well into his 70s and continues to support the campus in a variety of ways, demonstrates how sound a decision it was to offer him the position. Their shared year of service, the 1977–1978 academic year, helped to further solidify Torstenson's efforts and institutionalize Augsburg's commitment to experiential learning and its urban location. It also sparked a friendship between Hesser and the Torstenson family that kept them tied to Augsburg throughout Hesser's career.

LEADING THE CHARGE

Given that Hesser was hand-picked by Torstenson, it should not come as a surprise that both professors demonstrated commitments to many of the same goals and values. Like Torstenson, Professor Hesser cares deeply about educating students for democratic engagement at the intersections of place and mission, location, and vocation. While his accomplishments are vast, this section will briefly outline some of the key ways in which Professor Hesser used his expertise to help lead Augsburg's efforts in experiential education through tough economic times and constantly changing landscapes in higher education.

In 1998, Hesser published "On the Shoulders of Giants: Building on a Tradition of Experiential Education at Augsburg College" in Edward Zlotkowski's book, *Successful Service-Learning Programs: New Models of Excellence in Higher Education*.[4] Hesser argued that since Augsburg's 1869 founding as a ministerial training school for a Norwegian branch of the Lutheran Church, the institution has been committed to experience-based education. That history and tradition provided a firm footing for the expertise Hesser brought to Augsburg.

Before coming to Augsburg, Professor Hesser directed the College of Wooster's Urban Studies Program. The Wooster program was similar to the Higher Education Consortium for Urban Affairs (HECUA), with Hesser overseeing locations in Cleveland, Columbus, Detroit, Portland, and San Diego. While at Wooster, he also worked with the Great Lakes College Association's Philadelphia Urban Program. Perhaps most indicative of his commitment to students and their learning was the fact that while at Wooster, Hesser and his family lived with twenty students in a faculty-student community-service house. His graduate studies at the University of Notre Dame, during which he assisted the Office of Economic Opportunity programs in South Bend, also gave him skills that would ultimately shape Augsburg.

CONNECTIONS TO THE CITY

Because Torstenson transitioned Augsburg's Crisis Colony into HECUA and established a robust internship program in the Urban Studies program that was replicated in other departments, Hesser was able to begin his time at Augsburg by engaging in community-focused research. Tapping not only his research abilities but also his skills in cooperative education, Hesser trained several student researchers. Together, they interviewed over 500 residents of Minneapolis. The project examined the perceptions and behavior of central city residents concerning their housing and neighborhoods. Such an in-depth examination of his new city allowed Professor Hesser to quickly become a well-respected expert on the city of Minneapolis and its residents.

Hesser simultaneously became an expert on his new city through his personal life. Upon moving to Minneapolis, Hesser and his family rented a home in the Willard-Homewood neighborhood of North Minneapolis. The neighborhood was an urban renewal/model cities neighborhood led by Van White, who became Minneapolis's first African American elected to the City Council. While a resident of the racially diverse neighborhood, Hesser served on the Willard-Homewood Neighborhood Association and worked on Van White's campaign. After several unsuccessful attempts to purchase a home in the Willard-Homewood Neighborhood, Joel Torstenson helped the Hesser family locate a lot in the Seward neighborhood, located just south of campus. Seward was undergoing urban renewal and historic preservation efforts around Milwaukee Avenue, a planned worker community built in the 1880s to house the families of Milwaukee Railroad employees. As he did in the Willard-Homewood neighborhood, Hesser also shared his expertise by serving for decades on the Seward Redesign Community Development Board and with other neighborhood groups.

Like Torstenson, Hesser had the opportunity to partner with Joe Bash, co-founder of the Crisis Colony. Bash, clearly someone with multiple talents and interests, helped establish a community radio station serving Minneapolis's Northside neighborhoods. The station, KMOJ, was housed in a Minneapolis Housing Authority high-rise apartment building for senior citizens in the same neighborhood as the Crisis Colony. Early in his career, Hesser served as Augsburg's representative on the KMOJ Board of Directors. Through his work on the board, Hesser learned the apartment complex struggled to serve its older residents. Taking a page out of the Torstenson-Bash playbook, Hesser partnered with Bash to create a program that immersed Augsburg students in the community. The program ran for four years, with several students living rent-free in the building, serving on the residents' council, and co-facilitating community activities at a neighborhood community center. This community partnership foreshadowed the innovations in service-learning that Hesser would later develop at Augsburg. Examples like those just described highlight a few of the many similarities between Torstenson and Hesser. They were both influenced by and affirmed the work of John Dewey in integrating experiential education into Augsburg's curriculum; they were deeply committed to the integrated view of place and mission in the education of students; and if there was a way to learn more about an issue and to help the community, both professors found paths to do so that involved students in collaborative roles.

BUILDING AN INFRASTRUCTURE DESPITE ECONOMIC CONSTRAINTS

While financial constraints are not anomalies in Augsburg's history, the early 1980s brought particularly significant budget cuts and greater financial uncertainty. When institutions of higher education are faced with difficult financial constraints, budgets that do not keep the lights on and professors in the classrooms typically face drastic cuts. Throughout the 1970s, several programs, such as Augsburg's Metro Urban Studies Internship Program (MUSIP), were cut, so it would have been reasonable to expect that the continued efforts to create opportunities outside of the classroom for students—activities that take additional effort and expense—would have stalled. This was not the case for Augsburg's experiential education and service-learning initiatives. Because Augsburg was not always able to fully fund its commitment to experiential education, Professor Hesser, among many other faculty and staff, often carried out these initiatives by working harder, longer, and seeking outside grant support.

During the 1980-1981 academic year, Professor Hesser served as the Associate Academic Dean. That position included the responsibility of assessing Augsburg's internship programs. Like Torstenson's examination of experiential learning at other universities, Hesser collected information on other institutions, leading him to discover that Cooperative Education Title VIII funding could be sought to support internships. The availability of outside funding provided the opportunity for Augsburg to build a stronger infrastructure, hire staff that would become national leaders, provide paid internships for students, and involve more faculty in experiential education. In addition, Hesser and colleagues, including a group of students, faculty, and staff called the Augsburg Community Service Task Force, secured funding from the State of Minnesota and the federal government. Federal support came not only from Title VIII, but also grants from the Federal Work-Study program and the Fund for the Improvement of Postsecondary Education (FIPSE).

As an associate dean, Hesser was so successful at securing external funds to support experiential education that he was asked to serve a five-year directorship of the campus Cooperative Education Program. In this new role, he worked to ensure that experiential learning became deeply embedded into Augsburg's curriculum, staffing, and institutional structure. One of the most lasting impacts of Hesser's legacy has been the expansion of service-learning opportunities for Augsburg's students, faculty, and community partners. Hesser was able to expand service-learning not as a solo endeavor, but through two staff hires that were instrumental in implementing his vision.

Two main driving forces in Augsburg's evolution as a community of learners were staff members hired by Hesser, Lois Olson and Mary Laurel True. Lois Olson was hired in 1985 to initially serve as the Coordinator of Internships and Cooperative Education, but went on to direct Augsburg's Center for Service, Work, and Learning.[5] Upon her retirement, Hesser concluded that "no one has contributed more than Lois to the deepening of Augsburg's experiential education and career development."[6] Also contributing greatly to Augsburg's mission and leadership was Mary Laurel True, hired as Augsburg's first Coordinator of Community Service Learning in 1990. In that role, she quickly became the resident expert in incorporating service components into Augsburg courses as well as the unofficial liaison with the Cedar-Riverside neighborhood. For years, Mary Laurel was the first person to introduce new members of the faculty to all that the neighborhood and our neighbors had to offer.[7]

The expertise of Olson, True, and Hesser allowed Augsburg to further integrate service and community-based experiences into courses across the curriculum, even in some of the toughest economic times faced by the institution. For example, Olson and True served with Hesser on the Experiential Education subcommittee, which coordinated bookend experiential education experiences for students that have been integrated into Augsburg's signature curriculum. In their first year at Augsburg, students are introduced to the city through a course-based experience called "Engaging Minneapolis" and wrap up their time on campus after fulfilling the Augsburg Experience graduation requirement.[8] According to Hesser, "In all aspects of the experiential education program, there is a concentrated effort to create reciprocal relationships and mutual benefits among the three constituents we seek to serve: our students, the community, and the faculty and academic programs they represent."[9]

The invitation to serve as Augsburg's director of the Campus Cooperative Education program was an honor, but it did not come without sacrifice. Professor Hesser was planning to write a book with his College of Wooster research collaborator, economist George Galster. Both Galster and Hesser scheduled sabbatical leaves during the 1984–1985 academic year to focus on their large-scale research project on neighborhood development satisfaction among Ohio residents. In understanding the opportunities for more fully integrating internships and experiential learning at Augsburg, Hesser delayed his sabbatical and focused on what he determined to be best for the campus community. While a major sacrifice in terms of his research agenda, the decision ultimately led to Augsburg gaining national attention in two areas: experiential education and the scholarship of teaching and learning. As will be addressed in the following sections, accepting the directorship provided the opportunity for Hesser to pivot regarding his expertise and ultimately become recognized as an experiential education pioneer. The career shift also significantly reduced his time in the classroom for five years, which allowed Professor Diane Pike to be offered a full-time position in the Department of Sociology. The hire elevated Augsburg's reputation in a different area as Professor Pike ultimately became a national expert and leader in the scholarship of teaching and learning.

Hesser's creativity, urgency, and sacrifice were not just directed at the needs on campus. In yet another similarity to Professor Torstenson, Hesser was also deeply involved in supporting the Higher Education Consortium for Urban Affairs (HECUA). Hesser served on the board for over thirty years, including six years as President and four years as Vice President. When HECUA was on the verge of closing due to financial constraints, he volunteered to serve as an unpaid interim Executive Director (1992–1993) so the organization could regain financial stability. Had it not been for Professor Hesser, HECUA may not have been able to celebrate its 50th anniversary in 2021.[10]

IMPACTING THE EXPERIENTIAL EDUCATION CURRICULUM AT THE NATIONAL LEVEL

As a skilled sociologist, Hesser understood the complexities of institutional structures and proved adept at navigating the landscape of higher education amidst stiff financial constraints. Because of his efforts, innovations, and ability to professionalize Augsburg's commitment to experiential education as an integral part of the curriculum, the recognition and impact of his work went well beyond campus and HECUA. Torstenson's foundational work transformed the institution and its relationship with the city, and Hesser used that scaffolding to build a national reputation for Augsburg's innovative pedagogical pursuits. Through his efforts to professionalize Augsburg's staffing and the further integration of experiential education into the curriculum, Hesser became a sought-after expert and ultimately influenced thousands of professors and academic staff across the country.

Hesser's entrance onto the national stage started in 1985 when he attended his first National Society for Internships and Experiential Education (NSIEE) meetings. Augsburg was facing constricting budgets at the time, but he was able to leverage funds from the Cooperative Education Title VIII grant to attend the meetings. Professor Hesser stood out at the NSIEE meetings because there were very few faculty members in attendance. The meetings were typically attended by staff running experiential education offices on college campuses, but Hesser was there for a different purpose. Instead of learning about how to run programs as co-curricular experiences for students, Hesser brought with him a focus on experiential education as an academic exercise.

The fact that Augsburg's curriculum was closely tied to its intersections of place and mission, location, and vocation, garnered the attention of organizers as well as the Fund for the Improvement of Postsecondary Education (FIPSE) consultants in attendance. Five FIPSE consultants were charged with institutionalizing experiential education at twenty campuses. The goal of the program was to expand the efforts to train more consultants and impact more campuses. Hesser became part of the second group of trained FIPSE consultants and was asked to serve on the National Society for Experiential Education (NSEE, formerly NSIEE) Board. Within a few short years, Hesser was tapped to lead the organization, serving as the organization's vice president in 1986 and as a two-term president from 1987 to 1989.

Professor Hesser's leadership in NSEE certainly helped to bring Augsburg into the national spotlight, but what generated the most attention was his outreach as a FIPSE consultant where he promoted experiential education to thousands of faculty and staff. Through NSEE, he helped to create Experiential Education 101 workshops for those new to experiential education, in addition to developing learning opportunities for more experienced faculty and staff. The workshops Hesser helped build evolved into NSEE's Experiential Education Academy (EEA), an accredited certificate program consisting of a series of workshops. In keeping with Hesser's understanding and adaptability around financial constraints, he helped to build the EEA so that the certificate could be secured by completing eight workshops that were made available during NSEE annual conferences.

In addition to working closely with NSEE, Hesser contributed to efforts of the American Association of Higher Education and played a significant role in the Council of Independent Colleges (CIC) efforts to promote service-learning integration in the curriculum of member institutions. Professor Hesser also helped to create an organization designed to help Minnesota colleges and universities fulfill the public purpose of higher education. Similar to the way HECUA began to take shape in meetings at Augsburg with Joel Torstenson, Hesser and John Wallace, a philosophy professor at the University of Minnesota, hosted an on-campus dinner that eventually led to the formation of Minnesota Campus Compact.[11] Hesser and Wallace continued to support the work of Minnesota Campus Compact by helping the organization create a collection of syllabi from courses offering service learning, as well as offering countless faculty development workshops. Through a combination of venues and organizations, Professor Hesser led over eighty workshops across the United States and Canada.

Professor Hesser's work was not only external-facing, as he spent decades providing faculty and staff development opportunities at Augsburg University. In addition to actively promoting experiential education and service-learning through workshops and demonstrations, he also helped shape institutional policies. He was even able to bring Joel Torstenson back into the mix twenty years after his retirement. Professors Hesser and Torstenson worked with several faculty and staff to create Teaching and Learning at Augsburg College: Experience at the Core in 1998. The report, a product of Augsburg's Commission on Experiential Pedagogies, served as a formal invitation for the campus community to "engage in a dialogue about the best practices that lead to engaged learning."[12]

Given his tenure and the variety of his contributions to higher education, Hesser has undeniably impacted the curriculum at hundreds of institutions and the pedagogies of legions of faculty members. As a result, he has been honored by several organizations. The National Society for Experiential Education honored him as a Pioneer in Experiential Education (1998), with the Duley Lifetime Achievement Award (2012), as a Distinguished Scholar (2016), and most recently recognized with the Michael Steuerman Distinguished Service Award (2019). The Steuerman award is only given occasionally to those identified as leaving a lasting impression on the society and its members. NSEE was not the only organization to recognize Hesser's impact on higher education. He was also awarded Campus Compact's Ehrlich Award for Community Engagement (1998), was recognized as the Sociologists of Minnesota Distinguished Professor (2002), and was named the 2004 Minnesota Professor of the Year by the Carnegie Foundation for the Advancement of Teaching.

Interest in the curricular innovations at Augsburg was also generated through Hesser's scholarship. While his decision to delay his mid-1980s sabbatical derailed his initial research agenda on impressions of housing and neighborhood development in Ohio, his scholarship found a new direction. As a national leader in experiential education and service-learning, Professor Hesser contributed to several publications, most notably co-editing *Cultivating the Sociological Imagination: Concepts and Models for Service-Learning in Sociology* (1999), *Sociological Imagination and Service Learning* (2000) and the revision of the influential 1984 book, *Strengthening Experiential Education: A New Era* (2014). Regardless of the mode, be it his classroom teaching, professional workshops, administrative leadership, or scholarship, Professor Hesser rightfully earned being referred to as one of the Pioneers of Experiential Education. He was, without a doubt, worthy of carrying the Torstenson baton.

ENDNOTES

[1] Joel S. Torstenson, "The Liberal Arts College in the Modern Metropolis" (Unpublished position paper presented to the faculty of Augsburg College, 1967).

[2] Shortly after Torstenson's retirement, Congress passed the Age Discrimination in Employment Act (ADEA) in 1967, outlawing mandatory retirement before the age of 70.

[3] Torstenson's autobiography, *Takk for Alt: A Life Story*, demonstrates how active he remained in his scholarship and community service well into retirement. Joel S. Torstenson, *Takk for Alt: A Life Story* (Minneapolis: Self Published, 2004).

[4] Garry Hesser, "On the Shoulders of Giants: Building a Tradition of Experiential Education at Augsburg College," in *Successful Service-Learning Programs: New Models of Excellence in Higher Education*, ed. Edward Zlotkowski (Anker Publishing: Bolton, MA, 1989), 15–39.

[5] The work of the former Center for Service Work and Learning is now carried out in two of Augsburg University's Centers of Commitment, The Strommen Center for Meaningful Work and the Sabo Center for Democracy and Citizenship.

[6] Harry Boyte, "A Leader in Cooperative Education: Profile of Lois Olson," Huffington Post, January 22, 2013, https://www.huffpost.com/entry/cooperative-education_b_2491029.

[7] For more information about the contributions of Mary Laurel True, see Wendy Wheeler, "Neighborhood Resource Broker: Mary Laurel True," Augsburg Now, October 1, 2011, accessed July 31, 2023,
https://www.augsburg.edu/now/2011/10/01/neighborhood-resource-broker-mary-laurel-true/.

[8] Through the Engaging Minneapolis experience, first-year students explore what it means to study and live in a vibrant city. The Augsburg Experience graduation requirement can be fulfilled by activities such as internships, student teaching, field work, research, and studying abroad.

[9] Garry Hesser, "On the Shoulders of Giants," 28.

[10] On December 23, 2021, the HECUA Board of Directors, citing the financial impact of the COVID-19 pandemic, announced the immediate ceasing of operations. Augsburg University's Center for Global Education and Experience absorbed and continues to offer the Conflict, Peace, and Transition in Northern Ireland program.

[11] Minnesota Campus Compact (now Iowa and Minnesota Campus Compact) is a member of the National Campus Compact network, a national coalition of colleges and universities working to promote the public purpose of higher education through civic and community engagement in and outside of the classroom. For more information, visit https://iamncampuscompact.org/ and https://compact.org.

[12] Garry Hesser, Lee Hoon Benson, Carl Casperson, Terry Cook, Helga Egertson, Letitia Hooymay, Chris Kimball, Jim Trelstad Porter, Frankie Shackelford, Joel Torstenson, and Rebekah Valdivia, "Teaching and Learning at Augsburg College: Experience at the Core" (Unpublished internal report by the Commission on Experiential Pedagogies, 1998).

REFERENCES

Boyte, Harry. "A Leader in Cooperative Education: Profile of Lois Olson." Huffington Post. January 22, 2013. Last updated December 6, 2017. https://www.huffpost.com/entry/cooperative-education_b_2491029.

Hesser, Garry. "On the Shoulders of Giants: Building on a Tradition of Experiential Education at Augsburg College." In *Successful Service-Learning Programs: New Models of Excellence in Higher Education* edited by Edward Zlotkowski, 15–39. Anker Publishing: Bolton, MA, 1989.

Hesser, Garry, Lee Hoon Benson, Carl Casperson, Terry Cook, Helga Egertson, Letitia Hooymay, Chris Kimball, Jim Trelstad Porter, Frankie Shackelford, Joel Torstenson, and Rebekah Valdivia. "Teaching and Learning at Augsburg College: Experience at the Core." Unpublished internal report by the Commission on Experiential Pedagogies, 1998.

Torstenson, Joel S. "The Liberal Arts College in the Modern Metropolis." Unpublished position paper presented to the faculty of Augsburg College, 1967.

Torstenson, Joel S. *Takk for Alt: A Life Story.* Minneapolis: Self Published, 2004.

Wheeler, Wendy. "Neighborhood Resource Broker: Mary Laurel True." *Augsburg Now*, October 1, 2011. Accessed July 31, 2023. https://www.augsburg.edu/now/2011/10/01/neighborhood-resource-broker-mary-laureltru/

CHAPTER 4

Innovation, Inspiration, and Insight: Stories from Experimental Education at Augsburg[1]

As described in the preceding chapter, building on the legacy of Torstenson, Professor Garry Hesser's dedication to and leadership in experimental education, service learning, and connection to place opened up tremendous opportunities for Augsburg in these areas. Through the Center for Service, Work, and Learning in the 1990s (later the Strommen Center for Meaningful Work and the Sabo Center for Democracy and Citizenship) dedicated staff and faculty deepened Augsburg's commitment not only to the metropolis of Minneapolis, but to the neighborhood of Cedar-Riverside. Thanks to the contributions of Mary Laurel True, Lois Olson, and countless faculty and staff, Augsburg has been able to grow strong partnerships with neighborhood organizations, community leaders, and residents of Cedar-Riverside. These partnerships over the years led to opportunities for unique community-based learning and research opportunities for students, sharing campus resources with community groups and local residents, innovative collaborations to address community needs, and space for organizing and mutual understanding in a neighborhood that rapidly changed with the influx of East African immigrants and refugees in the 1990s and 2000s.[2]

In addition to laying the groundwork for place-based relationships and institutional connection to place, Torstenson's creative vision and its continuation through Hesser's leadership also made it possible for tremendous curricular innovations in the classroom connecting student learning with experiences far beyond campus, Cedar-Riverside, and even Minneapolis. From biology to political science to art: faculty and students are digging into learning that spills over the page and out of the lecture hall into relationships and applications with real-world impact.

In this chapter, we'll explore myriad examples of these innovations. In addition to descriptions of this work, current students and alums of Augsburg share how these unique learning experiences impacted their perspectives, educational path, and careers.

EXPERIENTIAL EDUCATION:
PLACE–BASED COMMITMENTS

From day one of student experiences at Augsburg, building relationships with and in the place where Augsburg is located has been paramount. For over twenty-five years, students have started off their Augsburg education with City Engagement Day (formerly City Service Day). Along with their professor and classmates from their first-year seminar ("AugSem"), students go out into the community for the afternoon to complete projects at community organizations. Each AugSem has a disciplinary focus, and each City Engagement Day site is carefully selected to pair with the discipline of the AugSem. The afternoon serves as an introduction to the communities surrounding Augsburg and the city of Minneapolis more broadly, a key learning aspect for Augsburg students in their First Year Experience. For some students, City Engagement Day is a catalyst to seek out volunteer or internship opportunities with the organizations they visited. The City Engagement Day experience is an important step in student learning as they begin to recognize and articulate their role in multiple communities, and to demonstrate agency to create positive, informed, and meaningful change in the world.

Over the course of time, Augsburg used a variety of terms to describe curricular and co-curricular student learning experiences connected to internships, volunteering, and learning in off-campus community contexts. Such terms have included service learning, community-based learning, and experiential education. Scholars from across higher education engaged in this type of university-community partnership work have interrogated these terms at length.[3] As staff, students, and faculty continued to deepen their connections in Cedar-Riverside, the Sabo Center for Democracy and Citizenship began to use the term "place-based community engagement" as a descriptor for the long-term work and ethos of walking with (rather than just acting in service to) Cedar-Riverside. Place-based community engagement is defined as "a long-term university-wide commitment to partner with local residents, organizations, and other leaders to focus equally on campus and community impact within a clearly defined geographic area."[4] Engaging with stakeholders from across the university and neighborhood community, a place-based approach aims to enact real and meaningful social change through partnership and co-creative work.

In recent years, Augsburg has engaged with a cohort of higher education institutions from across the country who are similarly interested in deeply focused, long-term, and place-based community engagement work. Recently formed into a formal organizational network, the Place-Based Justice Network (PBJN) consists of thirty-five member institutions that participate in annual summer institutes, continuous learning opportunities, leadership retreats, and other activities focused on place-based community engagement in higher education.[5] Augsburg hosted the PBJN annual conference on campus in the summer of 2019.

As a network, the PBJN aims to transform higher education and the communities surrounding them by actually working to deconstruct systems of oppression through a place-based community approach. The values of the network emphasize anti-oppression, anti-racism, intersectionality, self-determination, and deliberative process. This move toward an explicitly anti-oppression framework is an important and unique shift in the field of university community engagement, and one congruent with Torstenson's vision for the "church related college in the city" which was committed to peace, human rights, and "the role of higher education in urban affairs."[6]

The next section of this chapter includes the stories of some central partnerships and relationships between Augsburg and the Cedar-Riverside neighborhood. While by no means complete, stories illustrate the far-reaching depth and strength of these partnerships, and the creativity, innovation, and leadership of students, community members, and staff and faculty. In these stories, the borders between Augsburg and Cedar-Riverside begin to seem not so clear; it is all one community rooted in and committed to place.

Figure 4.1
Students and community members gather for an interfaith discussion at Cedar Commons.

Augsburg University. Used with permission.

INTERFAITH @ CEDAR COMMONS

It's Thursday night in the Cedar-Riverside neighborhood. People stream into the lower level of the small cinder block building that holds the church offices of Trinity Lutheran Congregation on

the second level. A buffet of food from a local Somali restaurant is set out and includes lentil sambusas, chicken and rice, and Somali tea. The space, formerly a bookstore and vegetarian restaurant, was now the home of Cedar Commons, a collaboration between Augsburg University and individuals who work, study, live, and worship in the Cedar-Riverside neighborhood. On this particular evening, Augsburg students along with community members fill their plates and prepare to discuss the topic of the night: religion and violence. The intergenerational and multicultural group assembled comes from various core commitments: they are Muslims, Baha'is, Lutherans, Catholics, Jews, Buddhists, spiritual but not religious, seekers, and confirmed atheists. What they share in common is a desire to explore their core commitments and build relationships across differences. These Thursday evenings are Interfaith @ Cedar Commons, one of a set of collaborative initiatives taking place there, all of which seek to build community, deepen collaboration around common goals and equip community members for effective leadership.

When Cedar Commons began, some expected it to become a social service center. Instead, Cedar Commons sought to cultivate and support collaborative work where students and community members could come together around overlapping vision and mutual benefit. With a staff member from Augsburg's Sabo Center convening, teams of students and community members began to create programs and events, such as an open mic night, a mentorship program, training on leadership and community organizing, and a series of panel discussions connecting young people with local leaders. Cedar Commons also supported community groups, such as AA, youth and women's groups, and educational events.

One initiative that emerged early on was an interfaith gathering that began during Ramadan one year when Trinity Lutheran Congregation and a neighborhood mosque, the Islamic Civic Society of America/Masjid Dar Al Hijrah, decided to host an interfaith iftar. After a successful night with rich discussions and connection, a second dinner was organized, and then a regular interfaith gathering convened. Before long, the organizing team grew to include the leadership of Trinity Lutheran Congregation and Dar Al Hijrah, a Muslim couple, a Baha'i couple living and working in the neighborhood, a campus minister from the University of Minnesota, Augsburg's Muslim chaplain, and an evolving array of Augsburg students.

Out of these organic relationships grew an opportunity for unique experiential learning for Augsburg students. The Interfaith Scholars program, which began due to student instigation in the wake of the earthquake in Haiti in 2010, started as a co-curricular gathering and eventually became a course overseen by the Office for Campus Ministry, the Christensen Center for Vocation, and the Religion department that continues to the present day. While incorporating a rich academic component, the course also seeks to create a community of interfaith leaders through interfaith dialogue, public leadership projects that bring interfaith understanding to the campus community, and civic engagement. In the last five years of the program, the civic engagement component happened through the public work of Interfaith @ Cedar Commons.

By creating a structure that forgoes the traditional model of community service, and instead facilitates authentic relationships between Augsburg students and community members, Interfaith @ Cedar Commons presents a unique paradigm for a university-community partnership. Augsburg University, then, is not merely an institution that works with "the community" but is an integral part of the neighborhood ecosystem. One community member framed it this way:

> As someone who is a community partner, it's been really cool to see how much this partnership has made Augsburg feel like part of my community. I've never been to a class, hardly been in most buildings but now I've had hundreds of conversations with Augsburg people every year and when I think about my neighborhood, I think about Augsburg.

Similarly, students participating in Interfaith @ Cedar Commons find belonging through an authentic, diverse, intergenerational community. Both students and community members alike know that on the second Thursday night of the month, a group will gather at the Cedar Commons for food, meaningful discussion, and relationship building with others who may understand the world differently than them.

CAMPUS KITCHEN

Like many neighborhood community centers, Pillsbury United Community's Brian Coyle Center does it all: providing community gathering space, social services, youth programming, advocacy, food support, and much more. On any given weeknight at Coyle, you can find something for everyone in Cedar-Riverside. Elders practice computer skills, young adults play basketball in the gym, community leaders meet to plan a collaborative event, and youth gather in the Best Buy Teen Tech Center. Though you may not know it unless they're wearing Augsburg gear, you'll also find students and staff, being present in all those situations. And if you're there during dinner time, you'll find Augsburg's Campus Kitchen students sitting down to eat with youth as they all take a break from homework to nourish their bodies and their growing relationships.

Founded as a settlement house in the 1890s, the Center has gone through many iterations to reach its current form, including iterations of partnership with Augsburg that have been built on long-lasting commitment and rooted in deep, communicative relationships. Amano Dube, Director of Brian Coyle Center, sees the relationship as reciprocal. "Augsburg students learn a lot about the community from Coyle. Students also bring assets and knowledge to us. It's a two-way goal." Mary Laurel True, former Director of Service Learning and Community Engagement at Augsburg, sees the partnership's goal as "to be together in each other's lives and to mutually teach one another and share resources." True worked to connect Augsburg with Coyle "in as many ways possible and with as much depth as possible," for over twenty-eight years. "Coyle is our neighborhood center," she explained, "The goal is to be partners in every possible way."

Ties to Coyle were cemented through an internship program with the Twin Cities Area Urban Corps in 1972.[7] By paying students to work not just on Augsburg's campus, but also in the Cedar-Riverside neighborhood, Augsburg made an intentional choice to direct its financial capital into the community. When Urban Corps dissolved, Augsburg took on the contracts internally in order to continue working alongside the organizations, and students continued to work at Coyle Center (then called Currie Center).

One of the key ways that Augsburg and Coyle Center work together today is through The Campus Kitchen at Augsburg. The Campus Kitchens Project was a national organization with chapters on college and high school campuses across the nation. Augsburg, the fifth campus to create a Campus Kitchen, launched its program in 2003. Campus Kitchen partners with Augsburg's dining service to recover surplus, unserved food from the dining hall and incorporate that food into weekly meals to share with community partners in the three neighborhoods adjacent to Augsburg. Campus Kitchen also runs a student food shelf on campus, recovers food from local farmers' markets to distribute in Cedar-Riverside, runs Augsburg's community garden, and provides education on food and sustainability.

Figure 4.2
Campus Kitchen volunteers get ready to serve a meal.

Augsburg University Archives. Used with permission.

Campus Kitchen student interns and volunteers (mostly Augsburg students) bring dinner to Coyle four evenings per week, ensuring that youth have access to a meal after a busy school day. Depending on the desires of staff and youth at Coyle, during some semesters and summers, Campus Kitchen provides additional food programming such as cooking in Augsburg's Food Lab, making snacks from gleaned vegetables and foraged berries, tending the garden, and organizing weekly "Top Chef" competitions.

Beyond food-related programming, Campus Kitchen interns and volunteers connect and build cross-cultural relationships with youth. For former Campus Kitchen student leader Hsinku Lay ('20), building relationships with youth at Coyle was a powerful learning experience. He shared, "We'd sit down and enjoy food together and talk about things like soccer or basketball and find simple connections between our lives and their lives." Hsinku was able to share knowledge about what it's like to be a college student and "be a role model" for youth at Coyle.

For Augsburg students who aren't from the neighborhood, their time at Coyle often shifts perceptions of the neighborhood. One student who helped with meals twice a week for a Social Work course said she used to hear people refer to Riverside Plaza, the iconic high-rise apartment buildings across the street from Coyle, as the "crack stacks." She had never ventured the four blocks from campus to be close to the buildings, let alone gone past them to get to Coyle. As she built relationships with the youth and adults at Coyle, most of whom live in the apartment buildings, she began fiercely interrupting that narrative when she heard it with her friends and classmates. Because she shared meals and built relationships with these neighbors, she became an advocate for the inherent resiliency and community spirit of Cedar-Riverside as she also felt more comfortable being out and about in the neighborhood. After three years of living on campus in the neighborhood, she finally felt like a Cedar-Riverside resident:

All summer we have been cooking and serving meals for youth at the Brian Coyle Center summer program. In addition, on Mondays we helped teach gardening, cooking, and nutrition lessons to Brian Coyle's K–8th graders. The theme for the summer was Top Chef and each week we had a cooking competition and awarded three participants Top Chef of the week. Thanks to grant support from The Campus Kitchens Project, these students were able to bring home a bag of groceries and recipes to their families so they could recreate the meals with them...(I)n Top Chef we had a salsa competition where students were given a certain amount of fake money to buy the fresh ingredients to make their special salsas. The students had to be creative in making unique salsa while still making sure they had enough money to buy all the ingredients for their salsa. The kids had tons of fun making salsa and many of them were surprised how good their salsa turned out. For instance, a few students challenged themselves by putting less common ingredients such as black beans or pineapple in their salsa and still ended up loving it! We were really impressed that almost all the students liked their salsa—we learned it is almost impossible to make bad salsa from fresh ingredients! Throughout the summer we learned about a community that is different from our own. We realized how everyone in Cedar-Riverside seems to know each other and how connected they are to their community. Even though we were out of our comfort zone a little at first, we were able to make new friends and learn new things, not to mention becoming all-star dishwashers and building our resumes!

AUGSBURG HEALTH COMMONS

In the early 1990s, nursing professor Bev Nilsson witnessed the impact of social exclusion and marginalization on individuals living on the streets of Minneapolis. She felt compelled to take action. Inspired by the framework of social justice and nurses' abilities to respond to the crisis at hand, she partnered with leaders at Central Lutheran Church to create the Augsburg Central Nursing Center (more recently named the Augsburg Central Health Commons (ACHC)). In this nurse-led drop-in center, people are welcomed without condition to a shared space that fosters human connection on a human scale. Students and faculty develop relationships with guests that are built on mutual benefit, and expertise is de-emphasized in order to foster a shared journey of health. In these moments, students are able to learn skills needed to decode systems of oppression that create health inequities, and those who visit the space regain trust with healthcare providers that has often been broken in previous interactions within traditional care settings.

Since that time, this community-academic partnership continues to thrive and grow, especially given the challenges that have arisen due to the COVID-19 pandemic and the racial reckoning spurred by the killing of George Floyd in the nearby area in May 2020. For example, when the pandemic forced buildings

Figure 4.3
Augsburg Central Health Commons.

Augsburg University Archives. Used with permission.

to close and people to socially isolate, those engaging in work at the ACHC had to respond quickly and get creative. While keeping the community safe from the virus was a priority, so was making sure that people experiencing homelessness or who were marginally housed had places to access food, toileting, and resources in the cold winter months. Thus, Pastor Melissa Pohlman and nursing professor, Katie Clark, collaborated with others working with this community during the crisis, and with those experiencing marginalization themselves, and they found ways to not only keep the ACHC functioning, but expanded the ACHC work to include bringing food and water to nearby homeless encampments. This allowed for the partnership to deepen and demonstrate its ability to live out its commitments together, in moments unimagined.

The majority of students who have engaged in this space report that the experience was meaningful, and some have even reported that it influenced their future career path. One student who graduated in 2021 said,

Interning at AHC has inspired me to continue working with the marginalized. In my future career as a dentist, I now plan on working within a community health setting. I believe this is where my values and aspirations to make a difference meet the needs of the world. I simply would not have gained this insight from reading a textbook or even watching a film. This experiential learning and engagement was the key to further worldly understanding and a humanitarian mind-set. My aim is to use the conversations and insights from Health Commons to honor the experiences of the individuals I have had the pleasure of meeting. I couldn't be more grateful for my time with Katie and everyone at Augsburg Health Commons.

In the Cedar-Riverside neighborhood, another Health Commons location was created in 2011. Prior to the opening, community members expressed their frustrations at having their health experiences minimized, as providers rarely incorporated faith practices in caring moments and often lacked cultural humility. In particular, elders expressed wanting a place to go within the neighborhood that had healthcare workers who could be accessed free of charge, without time constraints or proof of need. Fast-forward to the current day, and there are now two Health Commons locations in Cedar-Riverside (HCCR) within the Riverside Plaza buildings, the same iconic housing complex mentioned previously. The partnership represents a collaborative effort between Augsburg University, M Health Fairview, the East Africa Health Project, and People's Center Clinics and Services. The HCCR partnership has had to respond not only to the pandemic and social determinants of health that are impacting the community members, but to a recent opioid crisis in the community. Any classes or health-focused services, such as swimming, cooking, or yoga, are created at the HCCR based on the expressed needs of those who access the space. Community ownership of the HCCR has been at the forefront of the partnership work, which is reflected in the HCCR leadership and staff. For example, over the course of its existence, the leaders of the HCCR have hired bilingual community liaisons (BCLs), who are people who live in the neighborhood themselves, who work as both interpreters for the nurses and doctors, but also organize and connect with the residents. The BCLs have become the true leaders of the HCCR and many of them have begun exploring academic opportunities to become community health workers or nurses.

The future of Augsburg Health Commons locations will continue to change and expand to reflect the needs and desires of the communities served. Students from Augsburg internship programs, such as the Lead Fellows and Christensen Scholar Interns, help organize and staff this location, while graduate nursing students help provide for the care requested. In addition, Physician Assistant graduate students have focused their coursework on addressing social determinants of health (SDOH), aiming for a future with health equity in Cedar-Riverside. The potential for this experience to shift students' worldviews and to influence care systems through placed-based learning has been tremendous.

STUDENT REFLECTION: *Isaac Tadé '21.*

"Raised in the rural towns of Walcott, North Dakota (population 300), and Windom, Minnesota (population 4,400), I knew I wanted to try life in an urban setting once I graduated from high school. Augsburg became my college destination as the small class size reminded me of home, while the prime location in the heart of Minneapolis provided greater networking opportunities on and off campus. As part of my experience at Augsburg, I had the privilege of working with the homeless population across Minneapolis at Augsburg Health Commons through the program's paired internship. This drop-in center is run by nurses, and functions under the values of hospitality and mutually beneficial interactions. There is no room for savior complexes. I learned to ask what the needs of the community are before I act on potential solutions, which has helped establish trusting relationships with people who welcomed me into their community. I noticed that oftentimes the most meaningful acts of kindness can come from simply listening to people's stories. Taking the time to have sincere conversations with a population that is otherwise cast away validates their experiences. Each interaction fills me with perspective and new insight into life on the margins, which is why I am very grateful that my Health Commons internship was extended, thanks to generous funding through the Strommen Center (Augsburg's career education and internship center).

My experience at Augsburg challenged me to put my faith and my values into practice for the good of others. Besides my work at Health Commons, I also had the opportunity to live out this confluence of vocation and service through volunteering weekly with Augsburg Campus Kitchen (ACK). By repurposing leftover food, ACK volunteers promote environmental sustainability and reduce food waste. Salvaged meals were prepared, delivered, and served to the Ebenezer Tower retirement community, just blocks from campus in Minneapolis. Nearly every Friday night, you could find me laughing, singing songs around the piano, and enjoying a sustainable dinner with the residents. One of few social outlets within the retirement facility, the dinners were a time when residents could express themselves and be noticed. Over the years this lighthearted service gave me the chance to build a multigenerational urban family. Undoubtedly, my four years at Augsburg have brought numerous opportunities to grow in different areas of life. I was fortunate to bolster skills and gain insights beyond the classroom that will allow me to be a well-rounded healthcare practitioner and citizen of the world."

EXPERIENTIAL EDUCATION:
CURRICULAR INNOVATIONS

The impact of Torstenson and, later, Hesser's efforts to expand the walls of the classroom has also inspired tremendous innovation in course development and teaching and learning models at Augsburg. Three examples in particular—the River Semester, Design + Agency, and The Science of Food and Cooking—demonstrate that across disciplines, faculty and students at Augsburg engaging in experiential learning and teaching are finding their worlds expanded and their knowledge deepened in profound ways. As we'll read in the following pages, curricular innovation in the science lab makes learning science for those uninterested in it accessible, fun, memorable, and applicable to students' futures; students learning about geopolitics see competing interests and needs in action while paddling down the Mississippi; and design students working with real-world clients have a chance to create solutions and tell stories that might not otherwise be told.

THE SCIENCE OF FOOD AND COOKING

Augsburg's Science of Food & Cooking was created in 2013 to deliver a unique educational experience for students looking to take a science course to complete their general education requirements. Most colleges have some sort of general education, liberal arts, or distribution requirement as part of graduation criteria. Students at Augsburg can satisfy these options in lots of different ways, including by simply taking an online or community college course. The challenge is to find a course that is compelling enough that students want to take it at Augsburg, and are willing to pay more and perhaps have more engagement with the course content. This is particularly important in the lab sciences where costs of offering courses are often higher due to equipment and staffing needs while many students have voiced apprehension about a required science course. Despite these challenges, the importance of engaging college students in conversation about the process of how science works and the power of evidence-based reasoning is critical. Broadly educated citizens will make decisions requiring scientific literacy that affect society at large. A course focused on something as essential as food, which incorporated practical experiential learning applications, meant students had the opportunity to make connections immediately with their day-to-day life—after all, we all eat!

The course was organized around three principles. First, honoring students' prior experiences and their stories was foundational to the course design. Secondly, the course drew on Augsburg's resources and history of experiential education. Finally, the course was also designed as a potential resource for other activities and classes on campus, providing added value to the overall general education curriculum of the institution. In building this course we were fortunate to have the support of 2013 Sverdrup Visiting Scientist, David Weitz of Harvard, who shared his experience from creating a similar course in 2011.

From day one, Food & Cooking was created to respect the student's attitudes about science. Most students come to college with a previous science course, many of which were negative experiences. This reality must be acknowledged along with the fact that students have many passions and vocations for other disciplines outside of the sciences. Faculty can't simply assert that "Science is Fun" or that students misunderstand their own experiences and feelings. Instead, we can take students at their word and work from there. A second way to respect a student's prior experience with science is to recognize that many students majoring in history, business, or music have already seen scientific equations and decided to study something else. A course that doesn't introduce new content or isn't in some way novel and engaging for all students doesn't honor a student's time. Students have broad backgrounds and abilities. Something in the course should be new, different, and interesting for every-one—this discourages bright and well-prepared students from tuning out because "we did this in high school." To counter these challenges, Food & Cooking applies traditional topics of physics and chemistry to the science hidden in our kitchen.

Secondly, the course was designed to leverage resources as a college in the city and our culture around experiential education, while respecting students' time and hard-earned dollars spent on their education at Augsburg. Food & Cooking does this by explicitly building moments in the course that are meant to spar-kle as an "Augsburg only" experience. The course should leave students with "moments" they can take with them for the rest of their lives, such as the "ick" of xanthan gum juice, making steak in class, or whipping mayonnaise by hand. These moments plant the seeds to re-contextualize future learning and experiences with food. These moments are also the basis for memories of "what they got from college." A memorable experience can give students a point of pride in their undergraduate experience. A cheese tasting or making steak can be the source of anecdotes and an understanding that the college experience was valuable. Simply, Food & Cooking was an effort to be something students would pay for without the distribution requirement.

STUDENT REFLECTION: *Ariel Gutierrez, '19*

"As a student, I didn't know what to expect when it came to registering for the Science of Food & Cooking course. I knew the course would blend science topics and food accord-ing to the reviews from students who had previously taken the course. As the class began and progressed, I noticed the con-tent could be applied to our everyday lives. In the class we were able to pay closer attention to chemical reactions and reasoning behind the occurrence. Previous to the course, these were reactions I saw happen but didn't know why. I was able to understand why avocados, apples, and bananas brown. Learned how to properly temper chocolate to make tasty treats and acquired knowledge of the different kinds of energy used to cook an array of foods. An example of this would be lime juice. We used lime juice to cook fish and make ceviche.

Fast forward two years after taking the course. As someone who is not great at cooking, I still use the material learned in class. I continue to pay close attention to the reactions of food and seek answers when I'm unaware of a reaction. Additionally, the class influenced the way in which I perceive food. I now think of the resources and energy it took for the food to grow, be processed, and cooked. And with no doubt I would take the class again and continue to learn about the diversity of meals out there."

Kane Balance, '22

"As a senior student who hadn't taken a single science course in college yet, it was a bit of a no-brainer for me to choose 'Science of Food & Cooking' as my only science class, fulfilling my course requirements. If I was able to predict ahead of time the most memorable lessons from this class once I finished, they would have had something to do with tasting the foods, or learning new recipes. In reality, the part of this course that stuck with me the most, was not the food and cooking aspect, but the actual science that went along with it. This class is very successful at tricking you into learning science, because I can tell you from experience that I am not the best at learning science, even when I try especially hard at applying myself. Though in taking Professor Stottrup's course, it seems that I was embedded with an over-abundance of scientific lessons which, yes, pertain to food and cooking, though they are happening in so many other aspects of life as well. I catch myself reciting these lessons in my head during everyday cook-ing encounters. Anytime I see a steak start to brown, I remind myself of the Maillard reaction. When I see the eggs go from runny to formed in the skillet in front of me, I realize that the proteins have been com-pletely denatured and will never go back to their original raw egg form. Being that I wasn't necessarily fond of having to take a science course due to general requirements, it is a huge surprise to myself just how much I've actually retained from his course. If you have the chance to take 'Science of Food & Cooking' before you graduate, you surely won't regret it."

To make an experiential education course—particularly a lab science class—sustainable, Food & Cooking had to focus on structural, logistical, and financial details. Logistical consider-ations that factored into the course planning included the needs of the broader university curriculum, course scheduling, cost, and when the course is offered. For example, professors might not think of curriculum as check boxes, but this is what many students experience. To make the course more accessible, the course was scheduled with multiple laboratory sections to pro-vide increased flexibility for students interested in the course. Most importantly, the laboratory experience was offered at half the instructional cost of other lab sections, without creating an undue burden on the faculty. Finally, although the course is popular enough to be offered multiple times per year, by offering it only once per academic year, the class enrollment is consistently maximized.

An exciting outgrowth of Food & Cooking was a tremendous resource for all of campus: in 2018 a food-safe laboratory known as "The Food Lab" was opened in Augsburg's Hagfors Center for Science, Business, and Religion. Other courses, co-curricular programs, and community groups now use the space in new and creative ways. For example, courses in Religion, History, and Environmental Science have all utilized the cookware that is sustained through the operation of the Food & Cooking course. Work associated with Food & Cooking has resulted in several co-curricular opportunities from organizations like Augsburg's Campus Kitchen, described above, which regularly holds events both that give students an opportunity to express their agency and explore a food as a topic in ways they find meaningful. Likewise, student groups use the space to hold seminars and talks while building community around food, or simply gathering to study. What started as a single experiential education class with a simple goal—give students a unique Augsburg experience while satisfying a core curriculum requirement—has sparked experiential education in other departments and created space for connection that was not present before.

Professor Ben Stottrup, creator of the course, writes: As an instructor for the course, learning from the students about their own food stories has been tremendously fun and rewarding. It is a joy to teach a 'required distribution type course' that students are excited about taking. Students have memorable labs and engage in material they are genuinely interested in learning. The course also has been professionally engaging for me. I get to teach about the same materials science I research. Through the course's engagement with local chefs, food scientists, restaurant owners, and food engineers I can grow professionally. Our faculty have described the course through the presentations at the American Chemical Society (August 2019) and Minnesota's

Association of Physics Teacher's Meeting (various), and even contributed a chapter in the *CRC Handbook on Molecular Gastronomy* (2021). I don't claim this course is great yet or has achieved its full potential. But it has generated significant goodwill and enthusiasm in our students towards science.

RIVER SEMESTER

In fall 2015, for the first time, a group of Augsburg students had the opportunity to travel by canoe down the length of the Mississippi River as part of the River Semester program. Taking courses in Environmental Studies, Biology, and Political Science, and undertaking self-designed independent study projects, the students immersed themselves (literally and figuratively) in the rich educational context of this iconic river. When faculty at other institutions learn of this unusual format, a typical response is that such a program would not be possible at their institution— an observation which raises the question of how it was possible at Augsburg. The roots of that possibility can, at least in part, be traced back to the work of Joel Torstenson. The River Semester

drew from and was supported by a number of Augsburg initiatives with roots in his work and sensibilities, including the Center for Global Education and Experience and the Center for Service, Work, and Learning (now the Strommen and Sabo Centers). The

Figure 4.4
Students on the River Semester navigate the waters of the Mississippi River.

Augsburg University Archives. Used with permission.

institution's entrepreneurial spirit, sense of obligation to serve the community, and sense of the educational opportunities such forms of engagement could provide created space for new programs responsive to circumstance and needs of the time. As such, the River Semester could be seen as a kind of vocational moment for a small, urban, Lutheran institution located a few blocks from the banks of the Upper Mississippi River.

The germ of the River Semester was planted in January 2001 as an Interim course on Environmental and River Politics. The on-water element of the program began with an initial six-day trip on the river in the Summer of 2001, as part of an expedition organized by the Audubon Society. These trips gradually grew in length and complexity until the semester program launched in 2015. The second 100-day trip took place in 2018, during a fall marked by record rainfall, flooding, and unusually cold weather. In 2019, in close collaboration with the Berlin-based Haus der Kulturen der Welt (HKW) and Max Planck Institute for the History of Science, the River Semester served as the connective thread for an extensive set of programs along the length of what was termed an "Anthropocene River."[8] The program continues to evolve, responding to the needs and priorities of Augsburg students, with an increasing focus on social justice and examining the histories of slavery and settler colonialism along the river. By 2021, having accumulated enough experience on the river, the program saw fit to make its own custom-made river education vessels. These sail- and paddle-powered catamarans are a new addition to the fleet of vessels plying the river and provide a safer and more comfortable mode of river travel. Even with the new boats, these are challenging experiences, with students traveling as a cohort for over 100 days, almost entirely outdoors, having to learn, study, and do homework with few modern conveniences and comforts of home. But the pay-off has been tremendous, with students reporting the experience as transformative and liberating.

Four graduates of the program—Emily Knudson ('15), Hannah Arvold ('17), Nell Gerhke ('19), and Steven Diehl ('20)—have all worked as field staff for the program. For each of them, River Semester opened up new possibilities and gave them a sense that there are different ways to learn (and live) than the norm. For Steven Diehl, the River Semester was:

> ... a long form meditation on place and people. Living for 100 days with the river and with others facilitates an embodied learning that is rarely found on campus. The immersion on the river reminded me to look closely, lean in, and see the stories and lessons that are all around ... To spend an entire semester with a group of strangers, living, and taking classes outside, and often unplugged from cell service, forces students to engage with one another in a more intentional way. We are all reliant on one another in a complex and intimate way and the community formed on the River Semester reminds us of this fact. The River Semester transcends traditional learning, teaching us how to be authentically and deeply engaged with places and with each other.

At a time when there is such an obvious need for changes in our society and economy, the River Semester attempts to model some of those changes, and in so doing, open up possibilities for students (and staff and faculty) to craft an authentic life. As Emily Knudson writes:

> One of the most profound transformations the river journeys have given me were the skills, theories, and space needed to live otherwise.[9] As I interpret it, life otherwise refers to straying from the capitalist and heteronormative path of success (marriage, house, children, money, etc.), and instead following new and uncharted routes. Other scholars living under the oppression of our mainstream, homophobic, racist, colonial systems have similar concepts for those who choose to live otherwise, such as Saidiya Hartman's waywardness as a beautiful experiment, or José Esteban Muñoz's leap towards a queer utopia.[10] Since I first paddled the Mississippi, I have bartended in Ecuador, come out as queer, worked on sailboats in the Caribbean, earned Masters degrees in Spain and Italy, lived in caves in the mountains of Andalucía, taught at a university in Brazil, and moved to New York City on a whim (and during a pandemic). This would have not been my

trajectory if River Semester hadn't given me the self-confidence to follow my wildest dreams off the beaten path.

DESIGN & AGENCY[11]

The ember of Design & Agency was sparked in fall 2015, with the idea by Art and Design faculty member Chris Houltberg for a collaborative exhibition entitled "Bittersweet: The Dark Truth About Chocolate." All students enrolled in Augsburg graphic design courses during that semester worked alongside Chris to contribute individually to creating the exhibition. The experience was a paradigm shift. Seeing students' capacities to address the political, social, and human layers of this issue not only reinforced the value of a liberal arts education but helped the students understand how they can position themselves in an active role as designers. They were engaged in designing a cohesive awareness campaign that could bring change on campus. The level of student motivation when contributing to something seen and experienced by the public was striking.

While this initial project was an experiment, it opened the door for many connections around campus. Chris began engaging staff and faculty that were already doing community-based learning. He discovered many resources dedicated to experiential learning and ultimately began to forge connections in the community through the staff of the Sabo Center for Democracy and Citizenship. Drawing on the foundation of Augsburg's mission, the knowledge gained from the prototypes as well informed by the many rich histories of community-engaged learning, and the vibrant surrounding community itself, Chris set out to design a new major around this model of education. The result was Design & Agency, a design studio embedded into Augsburg University's Graphic Design program. The structure is defined by professors working alongside students to mentor, guide, and collaborate with them to create meaningful design solutions for local and international community partners. The philosophy and structure of this model focus on two main areas: creative problem solving with the ability to adapt to constantly changing issues, and students practicing to access their own agency.

As a student-led educational experimental art and design studio, Design & Agency is a hub where students are mentored by faculty and other students to transition from passive, compliant observers to active and curious instigators. It's a physical space where students invite community members and organizations to listen, engage, and collaborate with each other to solve, present, and implement complex design projects. And it's an intellectual space where personal creative identities are nurtured, practiced, and advanced.

One case study which easily exemplifies this dynamic community-based client experience is Design & Agency's longtime client, Sisterhood Boutique.

Located on Riverside Avenue, just the opposite side of the street from Augsburg, Sisterhood Boutique is a modest corner storefront focused on the sale and resale of girls' and women's clothing. Born from the Brian Coyle Center Youth Entrepreneurship Program, participants decided to build something positive for girls and women in the neighborhood. The Sisterhood Boutique was connected with Design & Agency after they had collaborated with Augsburg's MBA program to write a business plan. The Sisterhood Boutique and Design & Agency teamed up to experience together the entrepreneurial energy of starting a business. The studio created the primary brand identity for Sisterhood Boutique in the first year, expanded the interior and exterior signage another, and designed the

Figure 4.5
Student designers from Design & Agency meet with Sisterhood Boutique staff.

Augsburg University Archives. Used with permission.

promotion for a full-scale annual fashion show the next. All the while, students in Design & Agency were collaborating, learning alongside, and gaining unparalleled real-world design experience with their clients.

Design & Agency has continued this work and expanded to over forty community partnerships. When students and the community are placed at the center of a working studio, the learning environment becomes more dynamic. Students connect to valuable skills such as active listening and empathy while developing additional skill sets that equip them to learn from others at the table and to provide unique and valuable contributions. Design & Agency extends the classroom into the community where real learning begins. As local citizens, there is a responsibility to move beyond the academic walls to impact the community around us. This is most evident when a student's skill set combines with the wealth of knowledge already in our community in a way that addresses a real need. There is a wide range of ways students can participate in their communities. Design can be a visible access point for students to see how their work can not only be experienced in the world but have a real impact on the community.

Blending community engagement with advocacy for students' individual creative voices allows for students to become confident in being voices for their own communities, which in turn shapes the broader direction of the studio as a whole. Such is the example of Olivia House '20 and her URGO (Undergraduate Research and Graduate Opportunity) project titled, "Where are All the Black Designers?", a research project focused on highlighting historically overlooked black graphic designers. This was a direct challenge to the canon of designers that Olivia was being shown in class, and points to exactly how we expect our student designers to act and think. "Design & Agency helped me see that I'm not a producer—I'm a designer. A designer who is capable of more than just designing logos, but of helping change even a piece of our world through the visual stories we create," said House. Design & Agency professor Chris Houltberg notes:

It was thrilling to witness the growth of the project. We were reading along with her to better understand the answer to her primary question and to reassess our own stories we were telling as graphic designer educators. The outcome far exceeded any expectations for the scale that was expected. She was approaching the research with form, story, and community in mind. "Where are All the Black Designers?" has since been sent to other design schools and organizations throughout the US in order to highlight this community of Black Designers, of whom Olivia is now a participating member. In response, we have since shifted our daily studio practice to include thirty-five percent self-initiated projects and sixty-five percent client-based work, so that students like Olivia can find their voice, point of view, and community all while designing for, with, and alongside the Augsburg community.

Joel Torstenson's vision of education pushed at the boundaries of learning and scholarship to include an expansive classroom and a broadened notion of where and with whom learning happens. Rooted in place and always connected to mission, these are just a few of the ways that Augsburg has taken the seeds of Torstenson's vision and expanded it in recent times into deep community partnerships and innovative experiential learning. As we shall see in the next section, these kinds of learning experiences not only offer a new way for students to learn and a connection between the university, its mission, and its place, but they also help shape student agency so that they are enabled to engage as citizens in the work of democracy.

ENDNOTES

[1] Material in this chapter includes contributions from faculty and staff contributors, present and past. We are grateful for the contributions from Augsburg colleagues Chris Houltberg, Dan Ibarra, Kathleen Clark, Natalie Jacobson, Rachel Svanoe Moynihan, Matt Maruggi, Joe Underhill, Ben Stottrup, and Steve

Peacock.

2 The Cedar-Riverside neighborhood where Augsburg is located has been a landing place for immigrants to Minnesota for over 160 years. Neighborhood demographics have changed over time; in 2010, over fifty percent of the neighborhood was of East African descent. See an online digi-tour of the neighborhood for more information: Anduin Wilhide, "Cedar-Riverside: From Snoose Boulevard to Little Somalia," accessed July 27, 2023, https://digitours.augsburg.edu/tours/show/1.

3 Corey Dolgon, Tania D. Mitchell, and Timothy K Eatman, *The Cambridge Handbook of Service Learning and Community Engagement* (Cambridge, United Kingdom: Cambridge University Press, 2017).

4 Erica K. Yamamura and Kent Koth, *Place-Based Community Engagement in Higher Education: A Strategy to Transform Universities and Communities* (Sterling, VA: Stylus, 2018), 19.

5 "Place-Based Justice Network," Seattle University, accessed July 27, 2023, https://www.seattleu.edu/cce/about/our-impact/advance-the-field/place-based-justice-network/.

6 Joel Torstenson, "The Church Related College in the City" (paper presented at the American Lutheran College Faculties Conference at Augsburg College, Minneapolis, Minnesota, October 3, 1974), 1.

7 Garry Hesser, "On the Shoulders of Giants: Building a Tradition of Experiential Education at Augsburg College," in *Successful Service-Learning Programs: New Models of Excellence in Higher Education*, ed. Edward Zlotkowski (Bolton, MA: Anker Publishing, 1989), 15–39.

8 Joseph Underhill, "Navigating the Anthropocene River: A Traveler's Guide to the (Dis)comforts of being at-home-in-the-world," Anthropocene Curriculum, Haus

der Kulturen der Welt, 2020, https://www.anthropo-cene-curriculum.org/contribution/navigating-the-anthro-pocene-river; Joseph Underhill, Anastomosis: The Many Mouths of the Mississippi River, Online Course, Anthropocene Curriculum, *Haus der Kulturen der Welt*, 2021, https://www.anthropocene-curriculum.org/courses/on-curricula/anastomosis-the-many-mouths-of-the-mississippi

[9] Macarena Gómez-Barris, *The Extractive Zone: Social Ecologies and Decolonial Perspectives* (Durham, NC: Duke University Press, 2017).

[10] Saidiya Hartman, Wayward Lives, *Beautiful Experiments: Intimate Histories of Riotous Black Girls, Troublesome Women, and Queer Radicals* (New York: Norton, 2019); José Esteban Muñoz, *Cruising Utopia: The Then and There of Queer Futurity* (New York: NYU Press, 2009).

[11] A team of students from Design & Agency designed this volume.

REFERENCES

Dolgon, Corey, Tania D. Mitchell, and Timothy K. Eatman. *The Cambridge Handbook of Service Learning and Community Engagement.* Cambridge, United Kingdom: Cambridge University Press, 2017.

Gómez-Barris, Macarena. *The Extractive Zone: Social Ecologies and Decolonial Perspectives.* Durham, NC: Duke University Press, 2017.

Hartman, Saidiya. *Wayward Lives, Beautiful Experiments: Intimate Histories of Riotous Black Girls, Troublesome Women, and Queer Radicals.* New York: Norton 2019.

Muñoz, José Esteban. *Cruising Utopia: The Then and There of Queer Futurity.* New York: NYU Press, 2009.

Seattle University. "Place Based Justice Network." Accessed

July 27, 2023. https://www.seattleu.edu/cce/about/our-impact/advance-the-field/place-based-justice-network/.

Torstenson, Joel S. "The Church Related College in the City." Paper presented at the American Lutheran College Faculties Conference at Augsburg College, Minneapolis, Minnesota, October 3, 1974.

Underhill, Joseph. "Navigating the Anthropocene River: A Traveler's Guide to the (Dis)comforts of being at-home-in-the-world." Anthropocene Curriculum. *Haus der Kulturen der Welt,* 2020. https://www.anthropocene-curriculum.org/contribution/navigating-the-anthropocene-river.

Underhill, Joseph. *Anastomosis: The Many Mouths of the Mississippi River.* Online Course. Anthropocene Curriculum. Haus der Kulturen der Welt, 2021 https://www.anthropocene-curriculum.org/courses/on-curricula/anastomosis-the-many-mouths-of-the-mississippi.

Wilhide, Anduin (Andy). "Cedar-Riverside: From Snoose Boulevard to Little Somalia." Accessed July 27, 2023. https://digitours.augsburg.edu/tours/show/1.

Yamamura, Erica K. and Kent Koth. *Place-Based Community Engagement in Higher Education: A Strategy to Transform Universities and Communities.* Sterling, VA: Stylus, 2018.

QUESTIONS FOR FURTHER REFLECTION

1. What are examples of place-based and experiential learning at your institution?
   How do students and faculty respond to these opportunities?

2. What organizations does your institution partner with to enhance curricular and co-curricular community engagement?
   What potential partnerships are you missing?
   What challenges exist to incorporate community engagement for your faculty? For your students?

3. One of the ways in which Augsburg gained notoriety was by leading efforts to bring service learning into the curriculum. More recently, critiques of service-learning have led to the use of newer terms perspectives such as experiential learning. What terms does your institution use for such learning experiences?
   Where do you see experiential learning efforts at your institution in the next ten years?

4. Professor Hesser discussed how experiential learning programs must benefit three constituents: students, members of the community, and the faculty and academic programs of the university. What are some ways your institution is addressing the needs of these three constituents?

PUBLIC WORK AND DEMOCRATIC PURPOSE:
INTRODUCTION

As with any vocational journey, Augsburg's community-engaged work is ongoing and changing along its path. We continue to imagine new ways of pursuing the work that Joel Torstenson charted for us: work at the intersections of vocation and location, of mission and place. Of particular note in this unfolding journey is embracing the university's broader role in what we call "public work," positioning the work of the university community in the context of claims for social justice and community-building.

The sixteenth century Protestant reformer Martin Luther's theological concept of the "priesthood of all believers" undergirds an institutional commitment to civic agency and democratic institutions, challenging the disempowerment that often characterizes traditional service-delivery models. Instead, we work alongside our neighbors in reciprocal and mutually beneficial ways, doing the "public" or "political" work that contributes to the collective agency of the neighborhood and community.

This public work is exemplified by Augsburg's current leadership roles in the "anchor institution" and citizen professional movements. Being an anchor institution requires Augsburg to demonstrate its commitment to being in relationships and partnerships with our neighbors and other organizations in ways that uplifts the democratic purpose of higher education as we work collectively to solve everyday problems.[1] This again demonstrates the uniqueness of what it means to be of this place, not simply part of the neighborhood that we physically reside within, but deeply engaged in the robust network of individuals, cultures, traditions, and ways of life. We draw inspiration for this work from the settlement house tradition, first organized in London and then established in New York and Chicago in the late nineteenth century, with its focus on place-based, democratic engagement.[2] For example, Augsburg is among almost two dozen colleges, universities, and healthcare institutions located along a light rail line linking Minneapolis and Saint Paul that have come together with neighborhood groups and civic leaders to understand how our self-interests as institutions can combine to create shared value for neighborhoods along the rail line. The anchor institution movement embraces this idea of shared value as a realistic understanding of how institutions can collaborate to serve broader public needs. Among our joint work as anchors of our neighborhoods are shared purchasing programs, supporting local businesses; workforce development initiatives, aimed at meeting the employment needs of institutions and residents along the rail line; placemaking efforts, focused on ensuring safer and more liveable neighborhoods; and community-based research projects, involving students and faculty in applied research addressing social justice concerns and strengthening neighborhood services.

Similarly, Augsburg has embraced the importance of educating students as citizen professionals, recognizing that the civic agency of our students must be integrated into our curricular and co-curricular programs. Citizen professionals are connected individuals, with a sense of civic identity who are interested in co-creating change through public work, and by building relationships that serve the common good. As we will see below, helping students develop as citizen professionals has been woven into courses at Augsburg in diverse areas such leadership, history, and nursing. Through strategies such as public narrative, students develop a sense of their civic identities, and critically think through connections not only to their coursework, but to their developing sense of vocation.

As a university in the city, Augsburg stays; we accompany and settle alongside our neighbors. We live and work in Cedar-Riverside, the urban neighborhood where we have been with our immigrant neighbors for more than 150 years. We are called to educate students here who are skilled, reflective, and committed to service. We are called to be neighbors here, to do acts of mercy and to make this a place of hospitality and mutual respect.

As we consider the future of this work at Augsburg, we draw upon and commend to others these four fundamental lessons:

(1) Ground this work in mission and strategy: Find the threads of your institutional saga that inform your community-based work and then ensure that both your mission and strategic plan name this work as central to your identity and daily work.

(2) Leadership matters, but so does what happens on the ground: Presidential leadership and advocacy for this work is important, but it is not sufficient if the commitment and work is not integrated across all aspects of the university's work, including curriculum, campus life, business practices, and community engagement.

(3) This public work requires a commitment to mutuality with neighbors: One of the temptations, unfortunately too often endemic to academic institutions, is the tendency to believe we know best how to respond to community challenges. This work only succeeds if it is grounded in mutually beneficial relationships with community partners. Those relationships must be built and sustained over time through consistent, intentional efforts to align our work together around shared interests and values. To engage in mutuality in this way, we must also be able to recognize and name the historical context to problems and issues that may arise through this work as we develop collective solutions. This cannot be accomplished without a deep sense of humility

and ongoing reflection.

(4) Finally, this is all about democracy—not as the machinery of government but as a social ethic: This is about living together with our neighbors, working to create more just, healthy, safe, and compassionate communities. And that only happens when we practice democracy in our words and deeds.

These lessons and movements will be further explored in Chapters 5 and 6 as we describe how Torstenson's model has rooted the university in its commitment to the common good, contributing to a healthy democracy, while embracing the opportunities that exist from our unique urban location. The constant transformation of the urban consciousness that he described has moved us into our most recent endeavors—a vision of the democratic purpose of higher education which requires students, faculty, staff, and community members to develop their civic agency to address problems of our times through collective actions as citizens of place.

ENDNOTES

[1] For an overview of the anchor institution movement in the United States, see MARGA, Inc. "What is the Anchor Institutions Task Force?" accessed July 26, 2023, https://www.margainc.com/initiatives/aitf.

[2] For more information about the settlement house tradition, see John E. Hansan, "The Settlement House Movement," Virginia Commonwealth University, accessed July 26, 2023, https://socialwelfare.library.vcu.edu/settlement-houses/settlement-houses/.

REFERENCE LIST

Hansan, John E. "The Settlement House Movement." Virginia Commonwealth University. Accessed July 26, 2023. https://socialwelfare.library.vcu.edu/settlement-houses/settlement-houses/.

MARGA, Inc. "What is the Anchor Institutions Task Force?" Accessed July 26, 2023. https://www.margainc.com/initiatives/aitf.

CHAPTER 5

Constant Transformation of
the Urban Consciousness:
Civic Agency in Higher Education

As demonstrated in the preceding chapters, Augsburg University has responded to the constant transformation in higher education in meaningful and community-focused ways. In recent years, Augsburg has had to respond to a new challenge as the value of higher education continues to be questioned by society at large, especially in terms of its ability to aid in creating a healthy, robust democracy, to educate students to become engaged civic leaders, and to contribute to the common good.[1] Colleges and universities have also had to respond to the challenges of ongoing political polarization, a world of misinformation, and the deepening distrust the public has of institutions. Higher education is well positioned to demonstrate that by working with individuals, students, and communities to build both individual agency and collective ability, the change needed to bridge these societal divides can be ignited.[2] The future of our democratic way of life depends on reclaiming our nation's civic health. That reclamation begins with cultivating engaged students as civic professionals who deeply understand the public purpose of their work, who value being in mutually-beneficial relationships, and who understand the value of individual and collective public contributions.[3]

As we understand Augsburg's work in this moment by reflecting on its past, it's important to acknowledge that Torstenson wrestled with similar democratic challenges during his tenure. Torstenson responded to the crisis surrounding Augsburg in his time by taking action. His constant effort to transform the urban consciousness of the university was rooted in asking how Augsburg could do better by reexamining the role of education in the context of the realities of his time, and by leading faculty, staff, and administration to engage in public work to promote social change and to bolster a healthy democracy. This chapter will outline the deep ways that Augsburg has carried forward Torstenson's interest in the democratic purpose of higher education in modern times through curricular innovation incorporating civic agency, public work, and civic professionalism. This meant educating students to understand that our place-based community engagements must involve our location in a way that pushes the definition of location beyond a physical sense to also include a deep, interwoven web of ongoing relationships of peoples, cultures, environments, partnerships, and institutions. By providing space for students to develop the habits required to engage in a healthy democracy, higher education can provide an antidote to the crisis of othering and polarization that is upon us.

SHIFTING TO AGENCY

Reflecting on the impact of Torstenson's teaching, research, initiatives, and leadership, it's clear that his work pushed Augsburg to continually lean into the challenges of polarization and political or communal divides. As we saw in Chapter 1, Torstenson responded to the disconnect between the institution and community as he promoted political activism and understanding of realities of the city. Both then and now, there is a tendency in the United States to shift to a more community-lessness society, where individual expertise and merits are upheld over working together for the common good. In contrast, Torstenson's roots in a tight-knit farming community, the peace movement, and cooperative living grounded him in an ethic of community, even as he lived through the evolution to the individualistic society that resulted from the urban, political, economic, and racial crises of the late 1960s and 1970s.[4] As named previously, Torstenson wove these beliefs into pedagogical approaches such as that of the Crisis Colony, a "live-in" educational experience within marginalized communities.

Torstenson's pedagogical innovations also led to the creation of The Conservation of the Human Resources Program (CHRP), which started in 1969. The CHRP model was a co-learning model of education in which students, teachers, and community members all learned together in a non-hierarchical educational setting. The model was innovative in ways unparalleled. Although the course itself resembled that of other university offerings, its environment was anything but traditional. The first course taught in this format brought Augsburg students and faculty to Stillwater Prison, where students, inmates, and correctional officers all took a shared course on crime and society. The professor, Cal Appleby, emphasized that all those present were engaged in teaching and learning from one another, including himself. He referred to his role as an "enabler for learning" rather than a "giver of knowledge."[5] This approach was similar to the educational model used in the urban settlement housing movement of Jane Addams, which remains a source of inspiration of curricular innovation at Augsburg in the present day.[6] This teaching modality set the stage for the modern day focus at Augsburg on building the agency of all those involved in a learning endeavor, allowing for all participants to develop their capacity to take action, and to engage in a democratic way of life necessary to continue to push against the individualistic tendencies of our time.[7]

As mentioned in Chapter 3, during the late 1960s and early 1970s, Augsburg focused experiential learning experiences upon "the reemerging affirmation of the work of John Dewey and others who insisted upon a new epistemology and the relevance of experiential education."[8] Torstenson's report from his sabbatical, "The Liberal Arts College and the Modern Metropolis," also was used in strategic planning efforts to reweave pedagogical engagements, curricular efforts, and

academic opportunities at the university. This work led to curriculum revisions and restructuring internship opportunities in ways that aligned with a public purpose and civic outcomes.[9]
The evolution of the language of experiential learning and community engagement now finds itself in the midst of striving to "do with." While "doing with" was a crucial practice to the work of Torstenson and others, it has not been named so explicitly at Augsburg until recent years. This commitment of doing "with" and of co-creation doesn't end with curricular activities or community engagement efforts, but is deeply rooted in social norms and campus life.

As demonstrated in Chapter 4, since momentous shifts in pedagogical approaches instigated by Torstenson in the 1960s, Augsburg has worked to foster student engagement through a robust set of democratic pedagogies and applied experiential courses. The campus culture consistently remains open to and willing to support various initiatives, whether they come from faculty, staff or students. Augsburg has likewise nurtured adventurous and unusual opportunities for its students, linked to local resources and a sense of place. This type of experience requires individuals to be citizens of place, who can, because of their educational opportunities in the heart of the metropolis, understand their global responsibilities and to take actions that are created through relationships to create a brighter future.

CURRICULUM AS AGENCY BUILDING

In 2014, the Sabo Center for Democracy and Citizenship was officially launched at Augsburg University to cultivate "a more equitable and democratic world where all people develop agency and power to shape their lives and communities."[10] The overall goals of the center include facilitating community connection both within and outside Augsburg, transforming public leadership to build individual and collective power, offering opportunities and workshops to learn civic skills, and integrating public work, the "self-organized efforts by a mix of people who solve common problems and create things, material or symbolic, of lasting civic value," in community engagement and educated experiences.[11] The core team of the Sabo Center, consisting of faculty, staff, students, and administrators, works to infuse organizing principles into the daily practices of the institution. For example, as leaders of the Sabo Center intentionally strategized on how to move experiential learning experiences and community engagements beyond a service model towards one of co-creation, they hosted a series of conversations on how to structure and offer such learning opportunities. Conversations began around evaluating shared governance, reforming Faculty Senate culture, establishing new benchmarks for Augsburg in an emerging "Civic Agency Initiative," and transforming the curriculum to embed the concepts and philosophies of public work.[12]

Purposeful connections between civic engagement, public work, and citizen professions have been at the forefront of curricular innovation. This has occurred in various departments and within initiatives both on and off campus. The departments of Education, Nursing, Leadership and others have engaged in curricular redesign while other educational opportunities have been offered through on-campus workshops, forums, and events. In addition, President Pribbenow has been involved in conversations and strategic initiatives at the national level as higher education renews its democratic purpose, such as his work with the Kettering Foundation, his writings for such groups as the Association of Governing Boards of Universities and Colleges, and his leadership in the anchor institutions movement such as with the Anchor Institutions Task Force and the Anchor Learning Network.[13]

Curricular development in this vein has often been inspired by the model of Public Achievement. In 1990, Harry Boyte, a well-known scholar of public work and civic agency, along with a team of organizers, began Public Achievement to teach young people citizen politics and the broader view of democracy which he had experienced as a college student in the civil rights movement's citizenship education program, called citizenship schools.[14] Citizenship schools were based on respect for the intelligence and other talents of everyday citizens, and were at the heart of organizing during the 1960s movement. The schools included voter registration and education, and more broadly, they emphasized developing civic agency, the capacity of people of all backgrounds to act on collective problems of all kinds.[15]

In Public Achievement, teams of young people work on issues of their choice in real world settings. They meet through the academic year, coached by adults, often college students, who help them develop achievable goals, learn to navigate their local environment, and learn everyday political skills and concepts. Based on core concepts of citizen politics, public work, and free spaces, Public Achievement illustrates "civic studies" in practice. In the language of social change literature, the program takes an "organizing" approach, investing in relationship-building and people's public growth, rather than the "mobilizing" approach common in social change efforts.[16]

In 2010, Susan O'Connor, who was the director of special education at Augsburg University, utilized Public Achievement when she wanted to try something different. "Special Education generally still uses a medical model, based on how to fix kids," she said. The field has produced an internal critique, disabilities studies, which questions such a medical approach based on positivist science. Dennis Donovan of the Sabo Center, along with O'Connor, and Donna Patterson, another faculty member, partnered with Michael Ricci and Alissa Blood, graduates of the Special Education teaching program, to design an alternative class for special education students at Fridley Middle School using a Public Achievement-style approach. Over three years the results were dramatic. "Problem" students, often mostly low-income and from underrepresented communities, who in many schools would be confined to their classes, became public leaders on issues like school bullying, healthy lifestyles, campaigning against animal cruelty, and creating a support network for terminally ill children. They built relationships and received recognition in the school and in the larger Fridley community. Their Public Achievement work brought them into contact with school administrators, community leaders, elected officials, and media outlets like the local paper and Minnesota Public Radio.[17] Meanwhile, Augsburg's Department of Nursing was also exploring means of educating students to transform the healthcare system through civic problem solving methods. In 2014, nursing faculty and leaders from the Sabo Center held monthly faculty development workshops to engage in conversations on how transcultural nursing (professional nursing practice grounded in cultural humility weaving in the principles of anthropology) and public work built on one another to promote democratic engagement in the community and within healthcare. Changes to the curriculum ensued. Coursework now includes teaching students how to participate in activities such as one-on-one relational interviews, formulating and practicing one's public narrative, identifying and creating free spaces, and power mapping.[18] This work expands into the community setting where these skills are practiced in partnership with the community. Students learn to think of themselves as citizen professionals in the community and apply these skills to their practice of nursing, which has expanded into a larger sense of public purpose. These curricular commitments in the nursing department have remained strong in the intervening years. The impact of the global COVID-19 pandemic, worsening health inequities, and the declaration of racism as a public health emergency has further ignited nursing students to become catalysts of change.

Throughout these curricular offerings it has become clear that Augsburg offers a different kind of education, one that continues to strengthen social tapestries by creating a different kind of student: a citizen professional. Citizen professionals are deeply connected individuals who co-create change through public work that is both meaningful and timely. They realize the importance of deemphasizing models that rely on experts, instead forming purposeful relationships that serve the common good and practice social justice.[19] To become a citizen professional, students must develop their own civic identities as they begin to understand that in order to create change, they must work to overcome the polarizing and blame-based narratives society has become accustomed to. Additionally, the students must also not seek to "empower" other citizens or communities, but understand that power should be shared and leveled amongst peoples. It is vital that change emerges by building civic agency, both individually and as a collective.[20]

Developing students as citizen professionals means teaching students how to organize and use civic skills to address challenges and problems. This can be done whether programs weave themes of civic agency throughout their coursework or if it is offered as an individual class. Take for example, the curricular redesign of Augsburg's undergraduate leadership program. During courses and the final capstone project, students are introduced to the concepts and principles of responsible leadership and develop skills to enhance their ability to engage in public work. Students are introduced to the practice of public narratives and create their own. Gaolee Vang, a student in this major, shared with teacher Elaine Eschenbacher:

> One of my favorite activities we did over the course was the oral public narrative. The things that I talked about really came from the heart, it was raw and it was real. Something I found interesting was that I've never really thought about these things until I heard myself talking about it and I amazed myself too. It felt good to talk about the things I cared about. Then everything seems to make sense why I do what I do. I've never thought about how my story of us, self, and now, is a reason why I want to become a leader, it's fascinating how it all came together.

Professor Audrey Lensmire and Sabo Fellow, Minnesota First Lady Gwen Walz, have also incorporated the use of public narrative in their education course, "Connecting Policy, Practice and Advocacy for Education Equity." The course has two threads—analyzing the history of education reform through a critical lens and facilitating a process for students to develop their teacher identities by exploring their values, concerns, and passions as they too develop their public narrative. At the end of the term, students are asked to share their public narratives as a means to demonstrate their collective stories, values, and ideas on how to create needed change as future teachers.

In another example of helping students develop civic agency, history professor Jacqui DeVries drew on the problem-based learning model promoted by Civic Studies originator, Peter Levine, and used a real-world situation to help students understand a civic problem while asking, "What should we do?"[21] DeVries leveraged her relationships with a local history museum to engage students in civic agency and public work as they developed a walking tour of women's suffrage sites in the city, created an open access digital version of that content, and developed program guides, all of which was collected for Augsburg's library digital tours site.

Through these experiences, students learn to think of their chosen professions and vocations as woven into the life of their community and society.[22] Over the last few years, faculty and staff at Augsburg have developed means for students to archive their engagement both on and off campus in an electronic portfolio, called a V-portfolio (V for vocation).[23] This collection process is meant as an exercise for students to begin to understand their abilities, their strengths, and their self-interests throughout their academic journey at the institution in hopes of developing their holistic sense of agency. Current student Yasmin López said:

> Creating my Vocation Portfolio gave me the space to explore what I hold deeply in my heart, what matters the most to me; my portfolio portrays the social and political changes that my home country is going through, the scars of the past that as a community we haven't healed yet, and makes the process of getting to a democratic governance even more complicated.[24]

In conclusion, this chapter has provided some examples of how democratic purposes of higher education have been woven into coursework at Augsburg University and how this work is a continuation of the legacy of Joel Torstenson's innovative learning and teaching initiated in the 1960s and 1970s. As discussed, those who teach the importance of civic agency and public work must continue to use their passion and creativity to create pathways for students to develop a citizen professional identity, which cannot simply be manufactured through readings or academic endeavors, but must organically be developed by engaging in public work. While rooted in the inspiration of the past, Augsburg is looking toward the future to cultivate new and relevant ways to be a democratic university engaged in the community. This is especially demonstrated in its current efforts to create educational opportunities that allow students to understand their abilities, to learn the skills needed to create change, and to build relationships across differences, preparing them for civic leadership in a rapidly changing world that is rooted in Augsburg's commitment to mission and place.[25]

ENDNOTES

[1] Association of Governing Boards of Universities and Colleges, "Renewing the Democratic Purposes of Higher Education" (Washington, D. C.: Association of Governing Boards, 2019), accessed July 22, 2022, https://agb.org/reports-2/democratic-purposes/.

[2] Derek W. M. Barker and Alex Lovit, "Institutions and the Public: A Troubled Relationship?" in *Higher Education Exchange 2021 - Institutions and the Public: A Troubled Relationship*, eds. Derek W. M. Barker and Alex Lovit (Dayton, OH: Kettering Foundation, 2021), 1–5.

[3] Association of Governing Boards, "Renewing the Democratic Purposes."

[4] Joel S. Torstenson, *Takk for Alt: A Life Story* (Minneapolis: Self Published, 2004).

[5] Joel Torstenson, "The Church Related College in the City" (paper presented at the American Lutheran College Faculties Conference at Augsburg College, Minneapolis, Minnesota, October 3, 1974), 14.

[6] Torstenson, "The Church Related College"; Paul Pribbenow, "Lessons on Vocation and Location: The Saga of Augsburg College as Urban Settlement," Word & World 34, No. 2 (Spring 2014): 149–159. See the concluding chapter to this book for more about the influence of the settlement house movement on Augsburg.

[7] Catherine Bishop, et al., "Agency in Avalanche: Imagining Democratic Futures at Augsburg College," Unpublished manuscript, Augsburg University, 2016.

[8] Garry Hesser, "On the Shoulders of Giants: Building on a Tradition of Experiential Education at Augsburg College" in Successful Service-Learning Programs: New Models of Excellence in Higher Education

[9] Bishop, "Agency in Avalanche."

[10] "About," Sabo Center for Democracy and Citizenship, Augsburg University, last modified November 2018, https://www.augsburg.edu/sabo/about/.

[11] Harry Boyte, "Constructive Politics as Public Work: Organizing the Literature," Political Theory 39, no. 5 (2011): 632–633; "About," Sabo Center for Democracy and Citizenship.

[12] Bishop, "Agency in Avalanche"; "About," Sabo Center for Democracy and Citizenship.

[13] Association of Governing Boards, "Renewing the Democratic Purposes"; Paul Pribbenow, "Public Work and Higher Education in These Pandemic Times," Kettering Foundation, July 6, 2020. https://www.kettering.org/blogs/public-work-and-higher-ed-pandemic-times; Byron P. White,

"Toward the Community-Centric University," in *Higher Education Exchange 2021 - Institutions and the Public: A Troubled Relationship*, eds. Derek W. M. Barker and Alex Lovit (Dayton, OH: Kettering Foundation, 2021), 6–21.

[14] Bishop, "Agency in Avalanche."

[15] Dorothy F. Cotton, *If Your Back's Not Bent: The Role of the Citizenship Education Program in the Civil Rights Movement* (New York: Atria Paperback, 2012).

[16] Harry C. Boyte and Margaret J. Finders, "The Politics of Civic Agency and Education for Democracy (Agency and Activism)," (presentation, *Democracy and Education* Centennial Conference, Washington, D. C., April 8, 2016), https://docs.google.com/document/d/1-YxbraYRL2WtyyB_rmw8eEdz-2BqZI-xb/edit.

[17] Bishop, "Agency in Avalanche."

[18] "Public narrative," developed by Marshall Ganz, is a strategic way of sharing a story to inspire others to join in creating action with a shared goal or vision. See Marshall Ganz, "What is Public Narrative?" accessed February 16, 2023, https://changemakerspodcast.org/wp-content/uploads/2017/09/Ganz-WhatIsPublicNarrative08.pdf. "Free spaces" are public spaces where people can come together despite differences to engage in everyday politics or democracy. This engagement can take place through conversation or collective action. Many times, people referred to barber shops or front porches as free spaces during the civil rights movement. See Harry Boyte, *The Citizen Solution: How You Can Make a Difference* (St. Paul: Minnesota Historical Society Press, 2008). Power mapping "is a tool that helps to identify and understand the political and cultural resources that affect and are affected by an issue. It can narrow and clarify a complex and broad issue into something more concrete and workable" (*Clear Vision Eau Claire Coaches Manual, Clear Vision Eau Claire*, https://icma.org/documents/clear-vision-eau-claire-toolkit).

[19] Boyte, *The Citizen Solution*; Harry Boyte, Personal communication with Katie Clark, October 8, 2014.

[20] David Mathews, *Ships Passing in the Night* (Dayton, OH: Kettering Foundation, 2014); Kathleen Clark, "Treating an Ailing Society: Citizen Nursing in an Era of Crisis," in *Higher Education Exchange 2021 - Institutions and the Public: A Troubled Relationship*, eds. Derek W. M. Barker and Alex Lovit (Dayton, OH: Kettering Foundation, 2021), 36–49.

[21] Peter Levine, *What Should We Do: A Theory of Civic Life* (Oxford: Oxford University Press, 2022).

[22] Bishop, "Agency in Avalanche."

[23] Augsburg University, "Vocation Portfolio," accessed December 27, 2022, https://sites.augsburg.edu/vocationportfolio/

[24] Yasmin Lopez, "A Space to Explore," Augsburg University, accessed December 27, 2022, https://sites.augsburg.edu/vocationportfolio/reflections-and-testimonials/a-space-to-explore/.

[25] Bishop, "Agency in Avalanche."

REFERENCES

"About." Sabo Center for Democracy and Citizenship, Augsburg University, last modified November 2018, https://www.augsburg.edu/sabo/about/.

Association of Governing Boards. "Renewing the Democratic Purposes of Higher Education." AGB Reports, 2019, accessed on June 22, 2020, https://agb.org/reports-2/democratic-purposes/.

Augsburg University. "Vocation Portfolio." Accessed December 27, 2022. https://sites.augsburg.edu/vocationportfolio/.

Barker, Derek W. M., and Alex Lovit, eds. *Higher Education Exchange 2021 - Institutions and the Public: A Troubled Relationship.* Dayton, OH: Kettering Foundation, 2021.

Bishop, Catherine, et al. "Agency in Avalanche: Imagining Democratic Futures at Augsburg College," forthcoming in Timothy Eatman and Scott Peters, eds. *Rebuilding the Democracy College* (publication information forthcoming).

Boyte, Harry. "Constructive politics as public work: organizing the literature." *Political Theory* 39, no. 5 (2011): 630–660.

Boyte, Harry. Personal communication with Katie Clark, October 8, 2014.

Boyte, Harry. *The Citizen Solution: How You Can Make a Difference.* St. Paul: Minnesota Historical Society Press, 2008.

Boyte, Harry C, and Margaret J. Finders. "The Politics of Civic Agency and Education for Democracy (Agency and Activism)." Presentation, *Democracy and Education* Centennial Conference, Washington, D. C., April 8, 2016. https://docs.google.com/document/d/1-YxbraYRL2WtyyB_rmw8eEdz-2BqZI-xb/edit.

Clark, Kathleen. "Treating an Ailing Society: Citizen Nursing in an Era of Crisis," In *Higher Education Exchange 2021 - Institutions and the Public: A Troubled Relationship*, edited by Derek W. M. Barker and Alex Lovit, 36–49. Dayton, OH: Kettering Foundation, 2021.

Clear Vision Eau Claire Coaches Manual, Clear Vision Eau Claire, https://icma.org/documents/clear-vision-eau-claire-toolkit.

Cotton, Dorothy F. *If Your Back's Not Bent: The Role of the Citizenship Education Program in the Civil Rights Movement.* New York: Atria Paperback, 2012.

Ganz, Marshall. "What is Public Narrative?" Accessed February 16, 2023. https://changemakerspodcast.org/wp-content/uploads/2017/09/Ganz-WhatIsPublicNarrative08.pdf.

Hesser, Garry. "On the Shoulders of Giants: Building on a Tradition of Experiential Education at Augsburg College." In *Successful Service-Learning Programs: New Models of Excellence in Higher Education,* edited by Edward Zlotkowski, 15–39. Anker Publishing: Bolton, MA, 1989.

Levine, Peter. *What Should We Do: A Theory of Civic Life.* Oxford: Oxford University Press, 2022.

Lopez, Yasmin. "A Space to Explore." Augsburg University. Accessed December 27, 2022. https://sites.augsburg.edu/vocationportfolio/reflections-and-testimonials/a-space-to-explore/.

Mathews, David. *Ships Passing in the Night.* Dayton, OH: Kettering Foundation, 2014.

Pribbenow, Paul. "Lessons on Vocation and Location: The Saga of Augsburg College as Urban Settlement." *Word & World* 34, No. 2 (Spring 2014): 149–159.

Pribbenow, Paul. "Public Work and Higher Education in These Pandemic Times." *Kettering Foundation,* July 6, 2020. https://www.kettering.org/blogs/public-work-and-higher-ed-pandemic-times.

Torstenson, Joel S. *Takk for Alt: A Life Story.* Minneapolis: Self Published, 2004.

Torstenson, Joel S. "The Church Related College in the City." Paper presented at the American Lutheran College Faculties Conference at Augsburg College, Minneapolis, Minnesota, October 3, 1974.

White, Byron P. "Toward the Community-Centric University." In *Higher Education Exchange 2021 - Institutions and the Public: A Troubled Relationship,* edited by Derek W. M. Barker and Alex Lovit, 6–21. Dayton, OH: Kettering Foundation, 2021.

CHAPTER 6

The Way Forward:
The Intersection of Three Pandemics
and the Call for Leadership*

It was in the summer of 2020 when we all recognized that we were living at the intersection of three pandemics. The COVID-19 pandemic had disrupted all aspects of how we live and work, and pointedly illustrated the tension between public health and economic well-being. Following in the wake of the COVID-19 pandemic, an economic pandemic threatened our social fabric with massive unemployment and business closures worldwide. And, finally, the racial inequities exacerbated by the senseless murder of George Floyd by Minneapolis police officers created a third pandemic that threatened to tear our country apart. Surely this uncharted terrain presented unique challenges for all of us as citizens, trying to imagine how we would navigate to some as yet unknown future.

* *Versions of this chapter originally appeared in a blog post for the Kettering Foundation (July 2020), and as a chapter in a Council of Europe volume on higher education response to the COVID-19 pandemic (Paul Pribbenow, "Public Work and Reclaiming the Democratic Impulse of Higher Education in this Pandemic Times," in* Higher Education's Response to the COVID-19 Pandemic: Building a More Sustainable and Democratic Future, *eds. Sjur Bergan, Tony Gallagher, Ira Harkavy, Ronaldo Munck, and Hilligje van't Land. Council of Europe Higher Education, 25 [2020]. Used with permission).*

We experienced the intersection of these three pandemics with anger and resolve at Augsburg University, one of the most diverse institutions in the country located in one of the most diverse neighborhoods in the country. The impact of these pandemics on our students, faculty, and staff—and on the immigrant neighbors we cherish—was stark. Their health, their economic well-being, and their safety all were threatened. And we felt an urgent responsibility to act in response to those threats. This was an urgent call for leadership and action.

And there is much we did as a university community to accompany our community as we deployed our many resources to equip our community members to work on health, economic, and safety challenges. In fact, Augsburg University has, in its more than 150-year history, threads of democratic and public work commitments that shaped our efforts in those difficult days and months.[1] This, then, became an important moment for our university and all of higher education as we leaned into the impact of these pandemics with a powerful response grounded in our democratic commitments.

The democratic impulse of American higher education has called upon colleges and universities to reimagine how and what students learn, not due to the pandemics upon us, but despite them. We can no longer say that educational experiences should allow students to cultivate their own citizen professional identities as they learn to engage in public work and the issues of our time during their academic tenure, but they must. By allowing students to understand the importance of public life and to learn skills to create meaningful change—both within institutions and communities—they will learn how to contribute to a thriving democracy and become leaders of tomorrow addressing pandemics of the future.

There are a variety of pathways in the American system of higher education, each of which illustrates what might be called a "democratic impulse" in mission and purpose. It is an impulse that embraces a commitment to the integration of dignified work and citizenship for the well-being of our commonwealth.

It is an impulse present in the founding charters and in many forms throughout the history of these diverse institutions, and yet there also is evidence of how that democratic impulse has been eroded over the years—eroded both by institutional neglect and external forces.

For example, private liberal arts institutions were originally founded as "democracy colleges," meant to educate citizens to lead and pursue their work with a sense of purpose and dignity. Private research universities were organized as knowledge creators, contributing to the scientific and professional communities. And yet, in both cases, these institutions today are often seen as "elite" and disconnected from the communities in which they are located.

Another example are the American land grant institutions, chartered by the federal government in the late nineteenth and early twentieth centuries to pursue applied learning and community outreach, and yet now competing for rankings often based on metrics unrelated to the needs of the communities they serve. Or, consider our community and technical colleges, established after World War II to provide universal access for students to pursue vocational opportunities, and yet often buffeted by public disagreements about goals, funding, and mixed outcomes for students. In both land grant institutions and community colleges, the founding commitments to the dignity and centrality of work contributing to community capacity have been eroded, often replaced with an instrumental economic focus.

The point is twofold: the democratic work-centered impulse for higher education is present in the founding and history of institutions, and it also has been eroded and challenged to the point where that impulse may not be evident in the life of institutions today. At Augsburg, this democratic impulse is very much linked to the legacy of Joel Torstenson, and it is in that spirit that we renew the call for leadership to ensure our university will continue to be a beacon for democracy on campus, in our neighborhood, and around the globe.

As university leaders committed to the democratic impulse in the history of our institution, we believe that we must identify resources—especially intellectual resources—that can help renew that democratic impulse. The urgency of that renewal has been made more pressing by the intersecting pandemics of our time, each of which in its own way threatens the mission and work we pursue.

LESSONS FROM THE SETTLEMENT HOUSE TRADITION

One compelling source of those intellectual resources is found in the settlement house tradition, a tradition aligned with Joel Torstenson's vision of education at the intersection of mission and place. First, a bit of context.

The settlement house tradition, birthed on the east end of London in the late nineteenth century by Oxford-educated young people, sought to model how taking up residence in the midst of immigrant neighborhoods, engaging neighbors in exploring how best to respond to the realities of their lives, and then working cooperatively alongside each other to make the neighborhood safer, cleaner, and more just, could help solve urban problems and ultimately shape public policy to be more respectful of the value and dignity of work.[2]

In other words, "settling" in a neighborhood, becoming a neighbor, was seen as the most effective way to ensure healthier and more vibrant urban communities. This was in juxtaposition to the idea of "experts" coming into a neighborhood to offer and impose their solutions. The well-educated settlement residents certainly had expertise to offer, but it was offered in the context of neighborhood-wide engagement and participation. The lessons learned from these neighborhood efforts then became the impetus for social policies that would shape urban life for decades to come.

In the United States, the settlement house tradition took root initially in New York and then Chicago, where Jane Addams and her colleagues founded Hull House in 1889 on the near west side of the city and sought to transform a troubled immigrant neighborhood. Their work at Hull House—including educational programs, community centers, libraries, music schools, theaters, sanitation efforts, child labor practices, and honoring cultural heritages—illustrated the wide range of efforts pursued in response to the needs of neighbors, the richness of immigrant cultures, and the value and importance of immigrant work traditions.[3]

Although settlement houses were gradually abandoned, tenets of the settlement tradition took root in other forms in the late twentieth and early twenty-first centuries. As Ira Harkavy and John Puckett argued in 1994, the idea of applied sociology, which the early settlement leaders wrote about and practiced, offers a moral and pragmatic framework for colleges and universities to "function as perennial, deeply rooted settlements, providing illuminated space for their communities as they conduct their mission of producing and transmitting knowledge to advance human welfare and to develop theories that have broad utility and application."[4] As noted above, Joel Torstenson's curricular and co-curricular initiatives at Augsburg were very much designed at the intersections of rigorous scholarship and community engagement—applied sociology at its finest.

For place-based institutions like Augsburg University, the settlement house tradition (and specifically the work of Jane Addams and her colleagues at Hull House in Chicago) offers three key ideas that inform our response to the pandemic and help us renew the democratic impulse of our institutions.

1) DEMOCRACY AS A SOCIAL ETHIC

Democracy, for Jane Addams, was not simply a creed, sentiment, or political system, but an ethic that challenges us to balance individual needs and interests with the common good. In her book *Democracy and Social Ethics* (1902), Addams describes the idea of democracy as a social ethic with a simple image: we are all travelers on a thronged road, she said, and our minimum responsibility to each other is to understand the burdens we bear—in other words, to know each other's stories and circumstances.[5] That is the basis for a democratic social ethic. The genius of democracy is that the self doesn't go away, but it enters into relationship with others in mutual need and aspiration.

This is not a utopia, but a way of negotiating our lives together in a messy world. As we all recognize, things will not always go well, but with a democratic way of life they will go forward toward a horizon of shared purpose and dignified work that inspires and energizes our communities.

Similarly, in his book *With the People: An Introduction to an Idea*, David Mathews argues that "Democracy is us—The People. And we can restore our sense of sovereignty...by what we produce every day using the abilities and resources of our fellow citizens. And when the things that happen frustrate, disappoint and anger us—as they will—the question we have to ask ourselves is not what is wrong with democracy, but what are we going to do about it? That question can only be answered with one another."[6]

As universities committed to this idea of democracy as a social ethic, this "with" way of living together, we embrace the work we do—teaching, scholarship, and service—with a clear regard and a sense of humility about how we might do that work alongside our neighbors, who may not share our ideological, religious or political commitments, not apart from them.

This concept of democracy as a social ethic has informed our work as part of two "anchor" partnerships in our metropolitan area. In both the Cedar-Riverside Partnership and the Central Corridor Anchor Partnership, Augsburg University comes to the table with our neighborhood partners, stating our self-interest as an institution while we explore the potential for shared value for our neighborhood. Over the past decade, our anchor work has addressed neighborhood safety, workforce, youth programs, transportation, infrastructure, and place-making. The results are examples of how higher education institutions can lean into pressing community challenges as authentic partners, "with" our neighbors.[7] As noted in Chapter 1, our public work in the twenty-first century is informed by the Norwegian-American Haugeans who founded Augsburg in 1869 and believed deeply in the ways in which work and citizenship were inextricably linked.[8]

2) AN EXPANSIVE UNDERSTANDING OF KNOWING AND KNOWLEDGE

One of the most striking characteristics of the settlement house tradition was the embrace of various forms of knowing and knowledge. In this way, the settlement houses both helped immigrant neighbors assimilate to new surroundings, while at the same time helping them hold onto cultural practices and wisdom that might disappear in a new setting.

For example, at Hull House, Jane Addams recognized that certain ethnic and cultural craft practices were difficult to maintain without the materials and equipment to pursue them. In order to create opportunities to continue these craft practices, she created the "Labor Museum" where neighbors practiced these cultural arts and also passed them along to the next generation and neighbors unfamiliar with the practices.[9] This was a means of sustaining cultural knowledge and thereby enriching neighborhood life.

For colleges and universities, the concepts of what constitutes knowledge and ways of knowing are often limited to particular traditions such as the scientific method with its evidence-based claims or Western concepts of what constitutes truth and beauty. The settlement house tradition reminds us that there is knowledge and wisdom from many sources, and our openness to diverse forms of knowledge and ways of knowing has the potential to enrich our lives.

An example of this openness to different forms of knowledge for Augsburg is linked to our now regular practice of "land acknowledgments" at public events. We acknowledge that the land we occupy was originally settled by the Dakota and Ojibwe peoples, and we go further to lift up the ways in which indigenous peoples teach us important lessons—lessons we have forgotten— about how to be good stewards of the land. Knowledge and wisdom from native peoples expands and enhances our stewardship understanding and practices.

3) AN OPENNESS TO NEW SOCIAL ARRANGEMENTS

Throughout the history of settlement houses, a crucial strategy was to listen to the needs of neighbors and neighborhoods before organizing ways of responding to those needs. In other words, there was an openness to what I would call diverse "social arrangements," and there were no predetermined ways to organize.

At Hull House in early twentieth century Chicago, this sometimes meant a patchwork of organizational models as the needs of neighbors overrode any static, bureaucratic responses. A museum for labor and crafts here, a youth center there; a kindergarten here, a library there; a neighborhood sanitation team here, a safe labor practices group there. And perhaps most compelling about this openness to various social arrangements was the willingness of Addams and neighbors to admit when a particular arrangement did not work and search for a better option.[10]

For American colleges and universities, the idea of fluid social arrangements flies in the face of a fairly conservative, hierarchical bureaucracy, marked by many silos and layers, making it difficult to adjust to shifting needs. Yet, it is incumbent upon us to explore different organizational forms that create fluid boundaries within campuses and between campuses and the wider community, undoing the often privileged and static forms of organizational life that become obstacles for access and opportunity.[11]

At Augsburg, this openness to fluid social arrangements has taken various forms. For example, we have reviewed all institutional policies and practices through an equity lens, identifying where long-standing policies create obstacles to student progress and success. We also have partnered with various organizations to bring them as permanent residents to our campus. Based on shared commitments to education, civic engagement, and diversity, these partner organizations benefit from our organizational infrastructure, freeing them to use their resources more directly in areas of common interest, while the Augsburg community benefits from staff and programming that enrich our work in the community. Fluid organizational boundaries make it possible for mutual benefit in pursuit of common values and commitments.

RENEWING THE DEMOCRATIC IMPULSE OF HIGHER EDUCATION

So, we return to these fraught times, looking for evidence of this public work in our community—evidence that these settlement house tradition ideas make a difference. And here we find Professor Katie Clark from Augsburg's Nursing faculty, leading our Health Commons in the midst of the 2020 COVID-19 outbreak, meeting the needs of those in our community experiencing homelessness. And there we see our students, responding to a pandemic of systemic racism, putting their black and brown and white bodies at risk protesting for racial equity and law enforcement reform. And there we find our faculty and staff, seeing the distressing impact of unemployment and economic unrest in our immediate neighborhood, stepping outside of their daily routines to provide food and housing and security to our immigrant neighbors so at risk.

Surely there are a multitude of intellectual resources that might help inform how colleges and universities embrace their democratic work. Our examples have made a significant impact on our work at Augsburg and continue to shape our leadership. Our challenge to our colleagues in higher education is to (as we tell our incoming students each fall) show up, pay attention, and do the work, because our presence, our attention, and our public work are more urgently important for our democracy than ever before. Surely Professor Joel Torstenson would agree and challenge us to never step back from our radical roots, our commitments to the public purposes of higher education at the intersections of vocation and location, mission and place!

ENDNOTES

[1] Philip Adamo, *Hold Fast to What is Good* (Minneapolis: Augsburg University, 2019).

[2] Toynbee Hall, "History of Toynbee Hall," www.toynbeehall.org.uk/our-history, accessed June 22, 2020.

[3] Jane Addams, *Twenty Years at Hull House* (New York: MacMillan, 1910).

[4] Ira Harkavy and John Puckett, "Lessons from Hull House for the Contemporary Urban University," in *Social Service Review* no. 68 (1994): 312.

[5] Jane Addams, *Democracy and Social Ethics* (Urbana and Chicago: University of Illinois Press, 2002), op cit: 7.

[6] David Mathews, *With the People: An Introduction to an Idea* (Dayton, OH: Kettering Foundation Press, 2020), 34.

[7] Jay Walljasper, "Augsburg Deeply Involved in Innovative Effort to Keep Twin Cities Vital," Augsburg University, Blog—Office of the President, June 15, 2020, accessed June 22, 2020, www.augsburg.edu/president/blog/.

[8] Adamo, *Hold Fast to What Is Good.*

[9] Addams, *Twenty Years at Hull House*, 171–78.

[10] Addams, *Twenty Years at Hull House*, 109.

[11] Association of Governing Boards, "Renewing the Democratic Purposes of Higher Education" (Washington, D.C.: Association of Governing Boards, 2019), accessed July 22, 2022, https://agb.org/reports-2/democratic-purposes/.

REFERENCES

Adamo, Phillip C. *Hold Fast to What is Good: A History of Augsburg University in 10 Objects*. Minneapolis, MN: Split Infinitive Books, 2019.
Addams, Jane. *Democracy and Social Ethics*. Urbana and Chicago: University of Illinois Press, [1902] 2002.

Addams, Jane. *Twenty Years at Hull House.*
New York: MacMillan, 1910.

Association of Governing Boards. "Renewing the Democratic Purposes of Higher Education," AGB Reports, 2019, accessed on June 22, 2020, https://agb.org/reports-2/democratic-purposes/.

Harkavy, Ira, and John L. Puckett "Lessons from Hull House for the Contemporary Urban University." Social Service Review 68 no. 3 (1994): 299–321. https:// comm-org.wisc.edu/papers96/hull.html.

Mathews, David. *With the People: An Introduction to an Idea.* Dayton, OH: Kettering Foundation Press, 2020.

Toynbee Hall. "History of Toynbee Hall." Accessed June 22, 2020. www.toynbeehall.org.uk/our-history

Walljasper, Jay. "Augsburg Deeply Involved in Innovative Effort to Keep Twin Cities Vital." Augsburg University. Blog—Office of the President, June 15, 2020. Accessed June 22, 2020. www.augsburg.edu/president/blog/.

QUESTIONS FOR FURTHER REFLECTION

1. How is your institution's community engagement work grounded in mission and strategy?

2. What is the nature of your institution's approach to leadership of your community engagement efforts?

3. How and where does your institution practice mutuality with its neighbors?

4. What is your understanding of democracy and how do you seek to practice democratic engagement on your campus and in your local settings?

INDEX

164

ABOUT THE AUTHORS

GREEN BOUZARD is a freelance musician and editor. She formerly worked at Augsburg University in the Sabo Center for Democracy and Citizenship.

KATHLEEN CLARK, DNP is an Associate Professor of Nursing and the Executive Director of the Augsburg Health Commons. She earned her Bachelor of Science in Nursing from the University of Wisconsin Eau Claire and both a Masters of Art in Transcultural Nursing and a Doctorate of Nursing Practice in Transcultural Leadership from Augsburg University. She began her career at Augsburg in 2009 and has focused her scholarship and teaching efforts on caring for marginalized populations, developing experiential learning experiences to center the learning moments on people with lived experiences voices, and creating changes to address health inequities. She has led and expanded the university's efforts at the Augsburg Health Commons, which are nurse-led drop-in centers located in local communities that care for marginalized populations such as people experiencing homelessness, poverty, and immigration. Katie currently also serves on the Mission and Identity Division at Augsburg.

TIMOTHY D. PIPPERT, PH.D. currently serves as the Joel Torstenson Endowed Professor of Sociology and the Executive Director of Augsburg Family Scholars. He holds a Ph.D. in Sociology from the University of Nebraska and joined the faculty at Augsburg in 1999. He teaches a variety of courses from Introduction to Sociology to the Senior Seminar and Keystone and has published research on fictive kin relationships among men without homes, the accuracy of college and university photographic representations of diversity in recruitment materials, and the impact of the Bakken oil boom on the residents of northwestern North Dakota. In 2022, he worked with students in the Sociology Senior Seminar and Keystone to envision, design, and fundraise for Augsburg Family Scholars. The program, designed to support students with backgrounds in the foster care system, was launched in September 2022.

PAUL C. PRIBBENOW, Ph.D., is the 10th president of Augsburg University. Since joining Augsburg in 2006, Pribbenow has enhanced the university's role as an active community partner in its urban setting. By identifying and embracing initiatives that mutually benefit Augsburg and its neighbors, the university has achieved national recognition for its excellence in service learning and experiential education, including the 2010 Presidential Award for Community Service, the highest honor possible for service work. Pribbenow serves on the national boards of the Coalition for Urban and Metropolitan Universities (CUMU), Campus Compact, and the Council of Independent Colleges (CIC). He is also active in the Anchor Institutions Task Force, and chairs both the Cedar-Riverside Partnership and the Central Corridor Anchor Partnership in the Twin Cities. Pribbenow holds a bachelor of arts degree from Luther College (Iowa), and a master's degree and doctorate in social ethics from the University of Chicago.